More Praise for *Making Lemonade*

"A great strength of *Making Lemonade* is its respect for the early childhood workforce. This book is a feast of practical resources—easy-to-implement tips, adaptable classroom activities, lists of children's books, links to useful programs and lesson plans—all grounded in research and in the authors' broad experience and deep wisdom."

—Marilou Hyson, PhD, early child development consultant

"*Making Lemonade* systematically helps teachers to understand optimism, build a culture of optimism, and provides realistic strategies and tools to embed optimism as part of the classroom climate. I am positively sure you will love reading and experiencing *Making Lemonade*."

—Stephen P. Zwolak, executive director,
University City Children's Center, CEO, LUME Institute

Making Lemonade

Other Redleaf Press books by
Laura J. Colker, EdD, and Derry Koralek

High-Quality Early Childhood Programs: The What, Why, and How

Making Lemonade

Teaching Young Children to Think Optimistically

Laura J. Colker, EdD, and Derry Koralek

 **Redleaf Press**®
www.redleafpress.org
800-423-8309

Published by Redleaf Press
10 Yorkton Court
St. Paul, MN 55117
www.redleafpress.org

First edition 2019
Senior editor: Heidi Hogg
Managing editor: Douglas Schmitz
Cover design: Mayfly Design
Cover art: created by children at Eastern Ridge School, Great Falls, Virginia; photographed by Julie A.
     Liddle, atelierista and program director
Interior design: Mayfly Design
Typeset in Arno Pro
Interior photos by Peggy DeLanghe, Elizabeth Keller, Jessica Humphries, and Julie A. Liddle
Printed in the United States of America
26 25 24 23 22 21 20 19   1 2 3 4 5 6 7 8

Library of Congress Cataloging-in-Publication Data
Names: Colker, Laura J. (Laura Jean), author. | Koralek, Derry Gosselin,
  author.
Title: Making lemonade : teaching young children to think optimistically /
  Laura J. Colker, EdD, and Derry Koralek.
Description: First edition. | St. Paul, MN : Redleaf Press, 2019. | Includes
  bibliographical references.
Identifiers: LCCN 2018048157 | ISBN 9781605546612 (pbk. : alk. paper)
Subjects: LCSH: Optimism in children. | Educational psychology. | School
  children—Attitudes. | Learning, Psychology of.
Classification: LCC BF723.O67 C65 2019 | DDC 649/.64—dc23
LC record available at https://urldefense.proofpoint.com/v2/url?u=https-3A__lccn.loc.gov_201804
8157&d=DwIFAg&c=euGZstcaTDllvimEN8b7jXrwqOf-v5A_CdpgnVfiiMM&r=rvV70tfAjXVbLd
q1QdXNwJ7yH2gL-mOyODQS4d3gIYk&m=FQ-mUBXPGU54OPfXqwvuAxRtUalCupvhGVGK
QXTTBU8&s=9Fu1sqAJe7CMhs6vsucm8nvK_k_8Rpt07vxY3T7cVPE&e=

Printed on acid-free paper

To Doug, whose love and support would make anyone optimistic.

—LJC

To Craig, my essential partner on the road to optimistic thinking.

—DK

Contents

Foreword

The mission of the Life is Good Kids Foundation is to spread the power of optimism to kids who need it most—those whose lives have been deeply impacted by poverty, violence, and severe illness. We work toward this mission by supporting the people who dedicate their careers to building healing, life-changing relationships with the children in their care. We call these frontline child care professionals *playmakers*. In sports, playmakers make good things happen when the game is on the line and their team needs them most. We use *playmakers* to describe people who—at a pivotal time in a child's life—make a positive, powerful, and lasting difference. In other words, playmakers in sports help to change the outcome of games. Playmakers in child care help to change the outcome of lives.

As playmakers, we believe that optimism is the single most important trait that a child can have in order to lead a good life. Playmakers work hard to ensure that nothing destroys the optimism of children. Nothing.

But if you ask others what they believe to be the single most important trait that a child needs to lead a good, healthy life, optimism is not at the top of most people's list. I know this to be true because I've had the privilege and pleasure of posing this question to thousands of child care professionals from across the country and around the world. Traits like love, courage, compassion, and gratitude typically top the list. Is optimism really more important than love? Or compassion? Or courage? Or gratitude?

At the Life is Good Kids Foundation, we define *optimism* as a person's capacity to see and focus on the goodness in themselves, the goodness of others and in the goodness in the world around them. By this definition, optimism is a *prerequisite* for love, compassion, courage, and gratitude. Without the capacity to see and focus on the goodness in others, how can a person consistently act with love and compassion? Without the capacity to see and focus on the goodness in one's self, how can a person consistently act with courage? And without the capacity to see and focus on the goodness in the world, how can a person act with gratitude? Every positive, prosocial human trait is rooted in optimism.

Engineer Donald P. Conduto once said, "The most important thing is to keep the most important thing the most important thing." Optimism—in my experience—is the most important thing. The problem is that in times when we most need optimism, it is most difficult to come by. When we're feeling good and life is going our way, optimism—as an emotional state—is easy to muster. However, when things fall apart and life gets overwhelmingly difficult, optimism can dry up faster than a drop of water on desert sand. If we want optimism to be accessible to children even in life's darkest hours, we must help them develop optimism as a character trait and not just as a state of mind. Optimism as a state of mind is fleeting. Optimism as a character trait is lasting, and it requires three things—practice, practice, practice.

I am so grateful that Laura and Derry have written this book, and I am equally grateful to you for choosing to read it. This book—in addition to comprehensively exploring the topic of optimism—provides readers with very simple yet powerful activities designed to help nurture optimism in children so that it is available to them to whenever they need it. And as theologian E. Stanley Jones once said, "It is easier to act yourself into a new way of thinking than to think yourself into a new way of acting." If we as care providers are able to live life optimistically, we will be much better positioned to help the children in our care do the same.

Thank you for your interest in the wellbeing of children and for being intentional about building the type of relationships and environments that allow the seeds of optimism to take root and flourish. I can't think of a more important endeavor. For only when children feel safe, loved, joyful, and engaged in the present moment will they be able to truly see the goodness in themselves, others, and the world around them.

In closing, I would like to leave you with one final Life is Good pearl of wisdom: *There's no use being pessimistic. It wouldn't work anyway. ;)*

—Steve Gross
CEO and Chief Playmaker, Life is Good Kids Foundation

Acknowledgments

This book has been a long-time passion for us. As with most things of value, it came together with help from many caring and talented people.

At the heart of the book are optimism-related activities that were field-tested by a number of dedicated early childhood teachers. Their feedback allowed us to refine the activities and ensure they support teaching and learning optimism. We acknowledge and thank the following educators for their invaluable contributions:

- Shana Adoe, preschool teacher
- Sarah Bollingmo, site supervisor, Lincoln St. Preschool, Red Bluff, California
- Daniele Cooper, pre-K lead teacher, Princeton Children's Center, Wichita, Kansas
- Peggy DeLanghe, pre-K master teacher, Early Learning Center at Granger Community Church, Granger, Indiana
- Therese Fitzgerald, Sure Start teacher, Naples Elementary School, Naples, Italy
- Terri Granger, pre-K teacher, Department of Defense Education Activity, Johnson Primary School, Camp Lejeune, North Carolina
- Tonya Grant, early childhood educator
- Stacey Michalski, first-grade teacher, Kingwood Township School, Frenchtown, New Jersey
- Simona Moss, second-grade teacher, Kingwood Township School, Frenchtown, New Jersey
- Joanna Phinney, kindergarten teacher, Georgetown Day School, Washington, DC
- Cassandra Redding, Head Start teacher, College Gardens Elementary School, Rockville, Maryland
- Eileen Ricardo, kindergarten teacher, Kingwood Township School, Frenchtown, New Jersey
- Dawn Smith, preschool master teacher
- Terilyn Stephens, kindergarten teacher

- Katie Taffera, first-grade teacher, Kingwood Township School, Frenchtown, New Jersey
- Virginia Weaver, pre-K teacher and site supervisor
- Alicia Weeber, pre-K teacher, Seoul American Elementary School, Seoul, South Korea
- Allison Wood, associate teacher, TLC Preschool, Oroville, California

We are also grateful to our colleagues who helped identify and put us in touch with teachers: Colleen Badidas, Marcia Blom, Melinda Brookshire, Vincent J. Costanza, Rick Falkenstein, Marian Marion, Claudia N. Simmons, Mary Supik, Tyler Tescher, and Keith Young.

Finally, our thanks go to Julie Liddle, *atelierista* and program director at Eastern Ridge School in Great Falls, Virginia, and the children of Eastern Ridge whose optimistic art sets the tone for this book and its readers.

Introduction

Optimism. It's a word we all are familiar with. We know that optimists make lemonade when life hands them lemons. Optimists also expect things to turn out well, and they work toward creating positive outcomes. They persevere, even in the face of failures.

Optimism is a pragmatic attempt to give meaning to the events in one's life. It allows people to shape a picture of reality and respond in a way that seeks solutions and promotes well-being. Optimistic thinking is the skill of focusing on the positive without denying the realistic existence of the negative. It helps people channel their energy to focus on what they can control in their lives.

The best thing about optimism is that it can be taught and learned. So even those who aren't naturally inclined to think and act optimistically can learn to do so. Educators have shown that children as young as two and a half to three years of age can learn to be optimistic thinkers. And once learned, optimism makes a permanent, positive difference in a person's life. A child who thinks optimistically is positioned to reap the myriad benefits associated with an optimistic approach to life—beginning with doing better in school at all levels.

The study of optimism as a science (rather than as a curiosity) is relatively new. It is only in the last twenty-five years or so that researchers have been collecting data on the benefits of optimistic thinking. And because this research is so new, it is just now being reflected in early education. Professional development for early childhood educators has started to recognize the benefits of optimism on children's growth, development, and learning—not to mention the benefits for families and educators themselves.

Content

This book presents knowledge about learned optimism and suggests how to apply it in early childhood education settings, whether in classrooms or family child care homes. The information focuses on supporting preschool and kindergarten-age children, although it can be adapted for the early elementary years as well.

Chapter 1—Understanding Optimism highlights relevant research and our current understanding of optimism and its many benefits. It also shows the link between optimism and other positive educational practices: resilience, mindfulness, growth mindset, grit, gratitude, happiness, and kindness.

Chapter 2—Explanatory Style: How Optimism Is Learned introduces the concept of explanatory style and how to use it to explain life events to ourselves. The chapter focuses on how to use a five-step process to challenge a pessimistic explanatory style and make it optimistic.

Chapter 3—Creating a Climate for Teaching Optimism introduces skills and program-design techniques early childhood educators can incorporate to support children as they learn optimism. The targeted skills include emotional identification and regulation, executive function, confidence and self-efficacy, independence, perseverance, risk taking, problem solving, empathy, and self-calming.

Chapter 4—Activities for Building Children's Optimism highlights strategies for teaching optimistic thinking. We present twelve activities that can help preschool and kindergarten-age children develop an optimistic explanatory style. All the activities were field-tested in diverse classrooms, representing public, military, and private programs, including Head Start and the Department of Defense Education Activity overseas program Sure Start (which is based on the Head Start model). The early childhood education settings include those that are federally funded, state-sponsored, faith-based, and privately owned.

Chapter 5—The Optimistic Educator focuses on how early childhood educators can develop an optimistic explanatory style, just as the children do. By developing an optimistic explanatory style, teachers can be more effective role models and leaders, and they can also enjoy the benefits of optimism in their own lives. This chapter also addresses how administrators and other program or school and community leaders can support the implementation of learned optimism. They too can use optimistic leadership strategies in their roles.

Appendix A—Children's Books with Optimistic Themes is an annotated list of fiction and nonfiction titles appropriate for preschoolers and kindergartners. These books will likely lead to some interesting discussions about optimism and related concepts.

Appendix B—Tools to Help Families Support Optimism at Home includes a series of handouts that summarize the major tenets of optimistic thinking. Educators can reproduce these handouts for children's family members. In addition, there are adapted versions of six learning activities from chapter 4 that help families support learned optimism at home.

Appendix C—Learned Optimism Resources provides a list of books for educators and families who wish to explore more about optimism and related topics, such as resilience and mindfulness.

Audience

Whether you are a classroom early childhood teacher, a family child care provider, an elementary school principal, a child development program director or supervisor, a specialist, a consultant, a program developer, a coach, a trainer, or just someone interested in high-quality early childhood practice, this book will give you new insight on helping children learn to be optimistic thinkers. At the same time, it will provide strategies that encourage your own optimistic thinking and materials educators can use to engage families in their child's learning about optimism.

Taken together, these chapters and appendices include the tools and strategies needed to facilitate the teaching and learning of optimism. Optimistic thinking allows teachers to take fresh looks at their practices. It allows them to reflect on the "whys" behind the approaches they use to support children's development and learning. By doing so, every early childhood educator has the potential to change a child's thinking style for life and predispose all children for success and well-being.

We hope the information in this book will become well known in the near future, as teaching and learning about optimism become firmly ingrained in early childhood practice.

CHAPTER 1

Understanding Optimism

A pessimist sees the difficulty in every opportunity; an optimist sees the opportunity in every difficulty.

—Winston Churchill

What Is Optimism and How Does It Develop?

By definition, optimists are people who expect good things to happen—to themselves, to others, and to the world. Pessimists, on the other hand, brace for the worst. Considered both a character strength and a positive way of experiencing life, optimism affects our beliefs and our behaviors. Optimists approach problems with confidence and a high expectation of success. They believe that negative events are temporary, limited in scope, and manageable. In popular terms, optimists can make lemonade out of lemons and see a glass half-full, not half-empty.

From ancient times to the present, philosophers have pondered why some of us approach life with positive expectations while others expect negative outcomes. Only recently have documented answers emerged for this question. Much of the impetus and credit for this research base can be attributed to the emergence of the field of positive psychology in the 1990s. Positive psychology took the relatively young science of psychology in new directions.

For most of its existence, psychology focused on the treatment and cure of mental illness. By the close of the twentieth century, however, positive psychologists began turning away from the existing medical model that emphasized pathology and repair. Instead they shifted toward analyzing human flourishing. In other words, psychologists now examined not just what was wrong with people but also what was right.

Positive psychology, as explained by Chris Peterson, one of its founders, is the scientific study of what makes life worth living. He states, "Psychology should be as focused on strength as on weakness, as interested in resilience as in vulnerability, and as concerned with the cultivation of wellness as with the remediation of pathology" (2000, 45).

Positive psychology became popular mainly through the work of Martin Seligman, the current director of the Positive Psychology Center at the University of Pennsylvania. In 1996 Seligman was elected president of the American Psychological Association (APA). Positive psychology was the central theme for his tenure leading the APA. His mission was to validate the credibility of this new field. In Seligman's (2006, iv) words, "Psychology had told us a great deal about pathology, about suffering, about victims, and how to acquire the skills to combat sadness and anxiety. But discovering the skills of becoming happier had been relegated to amusement parks, Hollywood, and beer commercials. Science had played no role."

Optimism was one of the first and most important focuses of positive psychology. Around the turn of the millennium, an extensive number of research studies on optimism were conducted. This research radically changed the concept and understanding of optimism.

We now understand that optimists do not all don rose-colored glasses, whistle happy tunes, and use happy-face emojis. Nor do all pessimists necessarily look downtrodden, sulk, and curse the darkness. Optimism is a much more relevant and complicated construct than previously considered. Based on empirical research, we can now say the following about optimism:

- **Optimism and pessimism are best defined as ways of thinking.** Optimism and pessimism are rooted in the way we interpret what happens to us. Each of us has an explanatory style, a way to process both good and bad events. If we think a problem will have far-reaching, long-lasting effects, we have a pessimistic explanatory style. Conversely, if we believe a problem is temporary and has only localized negative effects, we think optimistically. An in-depth discussion of this topic appears in chapter 2.

- **Optimism is not a rigid trait; it leads to action.** Peterson and Bossio (1991) define optimism as "a set of beliefs that leads people to approach the world in an active fashion" (9). It should be noted that by "action," researchers do not just mean a general flurry of activity. Optimism implies deliberate, productive action. Optimists solve problems and make decisions that lead them to accomplish goals.

- **Optimism can be learned.** Because optimism is a trait, it is not fixed. And because it is a skill, it can be learned (Seligman 2006). Positive psychologist Susan Segerstrom (2006) writes, "Optimism is more what we do than what we are, and thereby can be learned. This has exciting implications for application and interventions" (167). Indeed, the fact that we can learn optimism may be its most powerful characteristic. It is the foundation for this book.

- **Optimists view failures as opportunities for learning.** It is said that the major difference between optimists and pessimists is how they view success and failure. Pessimists view failure as permanent, pervasive, and personal, while optimists see it as temporary, specific, and nonpersonal (Seligman 2006; Kamp 2013). As Albert Einstein observed, "A person who never made a mistake never tried anything new."

- **There is a gene for optimism.** Studies conducted in England (Fox, Ridgewell, and Ashwin 2009) and at UCLA (Saphire-Bernstein et al. 2011) identified an oxytocin receptor gene (OXTR) that is linked to optimism. Each of us inherits two versions of the gene— either two short ones, two long ones, or one of each. People who have two long versions are predisposed to be optimistic. As British researcher Elaine Fox states, "We've shown for the first time that a genetic variation is linked with a tendency to look on the bright side of life" (Sample 2009).

- **Optimism involves genetics and much more.** Although we have a genetic basis for optimism, genes alone do not predict whether we will become optimistic or pessimistic. According to Shelley Taylor, one of the investigators of the UCLA study, "Some people think genes are destiny, that if you have a specific gene, then you will have a particular outcome. That is definitely not the case. This gene is one factor that influences psychological resources and depression, but there is plenty of room for environmental factors as well" (Contie 2011).

- **Heredity only accounts for about 25 percent of our optimism.** According to Susan Segerstrom (2007), this figure is derived chiefly from a 1992 study of five hundred same-sex pairs of identical and fraternal twins. Half of the twin sets were reared together and half of them were separated at birth and lived apart. Researchers found that only one quarter of the traits of optimism and pessimism can be attributed to genes. The other 75 percent is determined by environment, social support, and learned behaviors.

- **The brain can be hardwired for learned optimism.** Because the brain can reorganize itself (neuroplasticity), learned optimism can rewire the pessimistic brain. Optimistic thinking patterns are primarily integrated into neural systems within the left hemisphere of the brain (Hecht 2013).

- **Optimism and pessimism are two separate constructs, not end points on a continuum.** Psychologists once thought that optimism and pessimism were opposite poles of a continuum and that people should strive for a realistic midpoint. We now know that optimism

I've missed more than nine thousand shots in my career. I've lost almost three hundred games. Twenty-six times I've been trusted to take the game-winning shot and missed. I've failed over and over and over again in my life. And that is why I succeed.

—Michael Jordan

and pessimism are two separate constructs. In some circumstances, both can coexist at the same time. That said, a high level of optimism is the most advantageous mode (Parashar 2009).

- **People are rarely across-the-board optimists or pessimists.** Because optimism and pessimism can coexist, most of us aren't totally wedded to one trait over the other. We can be mostly optimistic yet still be pessimistic about certain things. In certain circumstances, an optimist will act pessimistically and vice versa. For example, a person may be optimistic about his personal life but not his career (Peterson and Bossio 1991).

- **Optimism is constrained by reality.** Being optimistic doesn't mean being naive and blindly idealistic. Realistic optimism is about the ability to maintain a positive outlook without ignoring the negative. Realistic optimists acknowledge that problems exist, and they view mistakes as learning opportunities. They take responsibility for their actions, even when they go wrong. Realistic optimists do not automatically assume success. They know it will take fortitude, planning, and problem-solving skills to achieve their desired goals.

- **Most of us have a tendency to be overly optimistic in some situations.** This is known as "optimism bias," a phrase coined by Tali Sharot, a neuroscientist at University College London. Sharot (2012) believes that 80 percent of us have a tendency toward overly optimistic thoughts in some situations, even if we make a conscious effort to keep our optimism based in reality. For instance, most people hugely underestimate their chances of losing their job or being diagnosed with cancer. Also, most people think they are better-than-average drivers. Nearly every newlywed expects to live happily ever after. And what parents don't think their child is smarter, more talented, and better-looking than the average? But as Sharot notes, optimism bias isn't a negative attribute so long as we are aware of and compensate for it. It can, in fact, change our objective reality and act as a self-fulfilling prophecy.

- **Optimism is not a panacea.** Optimism predisposes us to be healthy; to do well in our relationships, school, and career; and even to live a long life. But there are no guarantees. Even if you train yourself to be optimistic, life isn't always fair and tragedies happen. What optimism can do, however, is help us cope with misfortune and reduce the accompanying stress. Optimism leads us to connect our dreams to our strengths. And it just plain makes life easier.

Are You an Optimist or a Pessimist?

If you're wondering about your own optimism, take the free fifteen-minute test at https://web.stanford .edu/class/msande271/onlinetools/LearnedOpt.html. See how well you know yourself. The results may surprise you. As you read the rest of this book, you will learn how to better understand the results.

Why Being an Optimist Is So Important

Research has not only helped us better understand optimism as a concept but it has also helped us understand optimism's extensive benefits. Optimistic thinking has a significant and meaningful impact on our well-being and success.

Many of the benefits of optimism described below are derived from research on adults rather than preschoolers and kindergartners. However, research and common sense confirm that growing up optimistically sets children on an improved life trajectory. The sooner one starts thinking optimistically, the easier it will be to reap the astounding breadth and depth of benefits that come from being an optimist. This is why learned optimism needs to be an important part of early childhood education.

Since the benefits of optimism also extend to you as you teach children and engage families, consider, as you read through this research, how optimism positively informs your practice, both personally and as an educational leader.

Optimism and Health

People with optimistic thinking styles have healthier lives, better survive serious illnesses, and live longer. In his landmark book *Learned Optimism*, Seligman (2006) lays out four ways in which research has linked optimism with general good health:

1. *Optimism strengthens the immune system, whereas pessimism weakens the immune system.* This finding has been validated by studies conducted in Denmark and by researchers at the Universities of Kentucky and Louisville (Association for Psychological Science 2010).
2. *Optimistic people are more likely to follow health regimens and seek medical advice than pessimistic people.* A Danish study of 607 patients

Optimism has clear benefits in the present. Hope keeps our minds at ease, lowers stress, and improves physical health. This is probably the most surprising benefit of optimism. All else being equal, optimists are healthier and live longer. It is not just that healthy people are more optimistic, but optimism can enhance health. Expecting our future to be good reduces stress and anxiety, which is good for our health.

—Tali Sharot, *The Science of Optimism: Why We're Hard-Wired for Hope*

with heart disease found that optimistic patients exercised more, adopted healthier lifestyles, and were 58 percent more likely to live another five years than pessimistic patients (Hoogwegt et al. 2013). A Harvard study (Kim et al. 2017) found similar results.

3. *Optimists are less likely to have illnesses caused by stressors such as divorce or job loss.* Optimists tend to be action oriented when facing and resolving negative events. Pessimists, on the other hand, tend to be passive. They typically avoid dealing with negative life events, and they often do nothing to stop them once they have begun. As such, optimists amass fewer negative life events and avoid the illnesses caused by them. In particular, the role of optimism in negating the aftereffects of divorce has been documented in studies done at Cornell and Oxford Universities (Karney 2010).

4. *Optimists have more social support than pessimists.* Isolation exacerbates illness, whereas engagement with others serves as a buffer against illness. In a ten-year follow-up study of 476 older men, optimism was found to be inversely correlated with loneliness and poor well-being (Rius-Ottenheim et al. 2012).

Life Expectancy

According to researchers, optimists live, on the average, nine years longer than pessimists (Reivich 2010). Perhaps the quintessential study on optimism and longevity is the Nun Study (Danner, Snowdon, and Friesen 2001). Researchers examined the two- to three-page autobiographies that 678 beginning nuns were required to write in the 1930s and 1940s. Specifically, the researchers analyzed the autobiographies in light of their optimistic and pessimistic content.

The nuns were nearly perfect subjects because their living conditions and environmental factors were controlled by their life choice: they had similar regularized diets, lived together in common surroundings, did not have children, and did not smoke or drink to excess. Thus the impact of traits such as optimism and pessimism could be readily studied without confounding variables.

The conclusion was indisputable and dramatic: optimistic nuns outlived pessimistic ones. The most optimistic nuns lived ten years longer than their most pessimistic sisters. By age ninety, optimistic nuns had a 65 percent survival rate and their pessimistic counterparts had only a 30 percent survival rate. Fifty-four percent of the optimistic nuns reached age ninety-four. Only 15 percent of the pessimistic-thinking sisters reached this milestone.

School Success

Multiple studies have concluded that optimistic children at all levels earn better grades, have higher test scores, and perform better academically than their pessimistic peers (Wray 2015). Pessimistic children tend to do poorly in school, have lower grades, and frequently suffer from depression as students.

A five-year study of four hundred third-grade children investigated the relationship between explanatory styles and depression. Investigators found the following (Seligman 2006, 144):

- If children started third grade with a pessimistic explanatory style and were not depressed, they became depressed over time.
- If children started third grade with a pessimistic explanatory style and were also depressed, they stayed depressed.
- If children started third grade with an optimistic explanatory style and were also depressed, they got better over time.
- If children started third grade with an optimistic explanatory style and were not depressed, they stayed depression-free.

Numerous studies of school-age children show that optimism is positively related to children's self-efficacy, problem-solving behaviors, and the ability to take risks and learn from their mistakes (Fischer and Leitenberg 1986; Seligman 2007). These are the same skills that enable preschool- and kindergarten-age children to thrive. Very young optimists are also more likely to do well in preschool and later schooling because they are better able to deal with its stresses, they have more social support, and they are more action oriented than their pessimistic counterparts.

Success in Sports

Optimism has been shown to have enormous positive effects on athletes at both individual and team levels. Because mental attitude influences success in sports, it's not surprising that an optimistic attitude would be an advantage to athletes. In talking about how explanatory style affects performance, Singer (2018) makes the following observations about optimistic tennis players:

> Optimistic athletes look at negative events as temporary setbacks, and as opportunities to actually refocus and crank up their performance during the rest of the match. They recognize that they have ultimate control over their internal dialogue and how they view negative events.... Even if they eventually lose the match, these optimistic thinkers understand how to change their internal

dialogue prior to and during their next match. Accordingly, these players will go into the next match expecting success and will usually win!

Research into baseball, basketball, and swimming shows that teams have their own idiosyncratic explanatory styles (Boniwell 2006). Teams with an optimistic explanatory style while under pressure or in the face of defeat are more likely to be successful in their next games. Optimistic teams try harder under pressure and perform better the next time.

Future Career Success

Optimists do better in their work lives and are more financially successful than their pessimistic peers. The same qualities that help optimists fare better in school and in health fortify them in the career realm as well.

To illustrate, a longitudinal study (Kaniel, Massey, and Robinson 2010) tracked the job-search performance of MBA graduates. The researchers concluded that "optimists are more charismatic and are perceived by others to be more likely to succeed." Here are some of the findings leading to this conclusion:

- Optimists experience significantly better job-search outcomes than pessimists with similar skills.
- Optimists are more selective in choosing positions and more likely to be promoted than others.
- Optimists are better able to internalize negative feedback on the job than their pessimistic peers and have better coping skills.

Positive psychologist Susan Segerstrom points to Amazon founder and CEO Jeff Bezos as the quintessential optimistic entrepreneur. She states, "Even when his [Amazon.com] stock was in the toilet and he was running his business out of his garage, he said he always had the belief that it would work out, and look where that got him!" (Seligson 2008) Today he is not only the richest person in the world but the richest person in modern history—worth an estimated $137 billion.

In sum, optimism benefits us in nearly every aspect of life. It sets us on a course of success and also makes the journey more pleasant and joyful.

Early Childhood Practices Related to Optimism

Now that you know what optimism is and why it's so important, it may be helpful to review the relationships between optimism and similar practices that impact the early childhood field. You have most likely read about or are applying some of these approaches in your program already.

Resilience. Mindfulness. Growth mindset. Grit. Gratitude. Happiness. Kindness. Most of these practices are outgrowths of positive psychology, and all have the goal of bettering lives. Consider whether you'd like to embrace some or all of these practices in your program along with optimism. All are compatible with the teaching of optimism, all can be learned, and all will enrich the lives of the children you teach and the families with whom you work. To learn more about these practices, consult the list of suggested resources in appendix C.

Resilience

Resilience is the ability to cope with adversity by persevering and adapting to the situation. It is the ability to bounce back from troubling experiences with a positive adaptation. Resilient people can handle life changes and challenges, such as moving to a new home or school. They are also more likely to get along with peers and try new experiences.

Some people—adults and children alike—seem to be naturally resilient. However, researchers have found that resilient individuals have common "protective factors" that allow them to handle difficulties:

> Do not judge me by my success, judge me by how many times I fell down and got back up again.
>
> —Nelson Mandela

- They solve problems, which gives them confidence to plan for the future.
- They have at least one caring friend or adult outside the family.
- They believe they have control over their lives.
- They are independent.
- They are sociable.

Research has identified seven critical abilities that boost resilience in children (Pearson and Hall 2017; Reivich and Shatté 2002). If children do not already have these abilities, teachers and families can support their development. These skills include the ability to do the following:

- stay calm under pressure and express emotions in a helpful way (emotional regulation)
- delay gratification and follow through on goals (impulse control)
- analyze the causes of problems (causal analysis)
- understand the needs and feelings of others (empathy)
- stay positive while accepting reality (optimism)
- believe they can persevere and solve problems (self-efficacy)
- take on new opportunities and connect with others (reaching out)

Optimism—the ability to stay positive while accepting reality—is one of the seven skills that boost children's resilience. The other six skills are closely related to optimism as well. Children who can control impulses, believe in themselves, and solve problems have an optimistic framework. Research has shown that teaching optimistic thinking skills is one of the chief ways of increasing resilience.

Mindfulness

> " Be happy in the moment, that's enough. Each moment is all we need, not more.
>
> —Mother Teresa "

Mindfulness is paying close attention to one's thoughts, feelings, and bodily sensations without making judgments. It can be practiced in everyday life, during nearly any activity. Mindfulness can help reduce stress, improve emotional regulation, enhance executive function, and increase attention.

Mindfulness is particularly suited to young children because it takes advantage of what is happening in their developing brains. During the preschool and kindergarten years, children rapidly develop connections in the part of the brain that governs focus and cognitive control. Children who are mindful can more easily focus on their daily activities and experiences.

Mindfulness can help young children reduce stress, be patient, pay attention, and use positive behaviors such as empathy, compassion, and kindness. It is also an effective technique for helping children develop optimistic-thinking skills. And with its focus on the present, mindfulness can combat one of the main aspects of pessimistic thinking—the tendency to focus on past and future implications of adversity.

Here are some helpful ways to teach mindfulness to young children (Tyrrell 2015):

- **Create a quiet space.** Designate a spot where children can pause and get used to the quiet. Point out how we may become aware of things around us in a new and different way.
- **Pay attention with purpose and curiosity.** Take a walk outside and encourage children to notice sounds of all types. Or have them try a mindful eating exercise. Instruct them to slowly, with quiet attention, explore a food item with all their senses before eating it. Have them notice the smells, colors, textures, and any sensations of pleasure or displeasure before actually tasting the food.
- **Pause and notice your breath.** Have the children lie on their backs and notice the movement of their chests or bellies as their breath moves in and out of their bodies. Other moments in the day—such as waiting in line—may be opportunities to bring attention to the breath as well.
- **Offer caring wishes.** Encourage children to practice caring and compassion for themselves and others. Start the day off by appointing a child to be a greeter who meets each person at the doorway with a smile, a handshake, or a hug, as requested.

- **Notice the good things in life.** Help children cultivate gratitude in simple ways. For example, invite the group to take a few minutes to reflect on the good things that have happened during the day. The group can keep a list of people and things for which they are grateful, or they can create gratitude journals using words and pictures.

Growth Mindset

A mindset is how we view our individual traits and skills, such as intelligence and talent. People with a "fixed mindset" believe that these traits are inborn and cannot be changed. This view limits learning, undermines determination, and hampers resilience. A child or adult with a fixed mindset thinks, "I was born clumsy and will be clumsy for my whole life. There's no point in trying to improve what can't be changed."

Individuals who have a "growth mindset," however, believe in working hard and sticking with a task or goal, even when it is challenging. They think that if they keep trying and applying themselves, they can eventually learn and reach their goals. This viewpoint creates a love of learning, and it also creates resilience. Researchers have shown that a growth mindset lowers stress and aggressive behaviors as well as promotes school success (Dweck 2014).

Carol Dweck, who introduced the term *growth mindset*, has spent many years studying the concept. She points out that in some instances, effort alone is not enough. Sometimes children and adults also need to learn the strategies that will lead them to success. Seeking support from others is one of those strategies. Dweck (2015, 24) states, "The growth-mindset approach helps children feel good in the short *and* long terms, by helping them thrive on challenges and setbacks on their way to learning."

Mindset leads to success or failure as well as determines whether we are optimistic or pessimistic. When a child with a fixed mindset tells herself, "I'm not smart," she views herself in the same ways a pessimistic child would. The goal of both growth mindset and optimism is to encourage children and adults toward healthy perseverance and success.

Teachers can discover many opportunities to promote children's growth mindset, including the following strategies (McKay 2015):

- **Explain that the brain works like a muscle.** Let children know that their brains will grow through hard work, determination, and lots and lots of practice.
- **Encourage effort and growth.** Avoid telling a child that she is smart or talented. Instead, notice and comment on her helpful actions and positive attitude.

> It's not that I'm so smart, it's just that I stay with problems longer.
>
> —Albert Einstein

- **Notice and comment on the learning process.** Help children see that effort, hard work, and practice allow them to achieve their true potential.
- **Explain that mistakes are part of learning.** There is nothing like the feeling of struggling through a very difficult problem, only to finally break through and solve it! Challenge children to see that the harder the problem, the more satisfying it is to find the solution.
- **Encourage participation and collaborative group learning.** Children learn best when they are immersed in a topic and allowed to discuss and advance with their peers.
- **Encourage competency-based learning.** Get children excited about learning content by explaining why it is important and how it will help them in the future. The goal should never be to get the "correct" answer, but to learn at their own pace so they understand the topic at a fundamental level and to want to learn more.

Grit

Grit involves perseverance and the urge to work on long-term goals. Children and adults with grit are likely to stick with a task until they reach the proverbial finish line. They keep trying to learn new skills until they master them. Grit helps a child return again and again to his long-term project—for example, making a paper puppy costume. It keeps him going until it's completed. Research suggests that when it comes to achievement, grit is even more important than intelligence (Quast 2017).

> " Grit is living life like it's a marathon, not a sprint.
>
> —Angela Lee Duckworth "

The four components of grit include growth mindset, self-efficacy (a belief in one's capabilities), personal control (believing that what we do contributes to certain outcomes), and optimism. Being optimistic helps children keep trying and sticking to their plans. Optimistic children see challenges as temporary setbacks that can be overcome. With grit, children can pursue their goals, succeed, and achieve.

Teachers and families can take many steps to promote grit in young children (Positive Psychology Program 2016):

- **Notice and comment on children's efforts.** This practice fosters resilience and growth mindset by reminding children of what they did that led to success. Use language that encourages perseverance and praises effort.
- **Model perseverance.** Let children notice what goals you are excited about and what you do to keep working toward them. They are likely to follow your lead.

- **Model creative and flexible thinking.** When you show that you are open and receptive to new ideas and ways of thinking, children will heed your example.
- **Help children break down a long-term goal into several short-term goals.** When children face long-term goals, it can seem daunting. However, by viewing goals as smaller steps that can be accomplished along the way to ultimate success, the task becomes manageable.
- **Encourage daily reflections.** Invite children to reflect about their day, thinking back on actions, conversations, and experiences. The reflection may take the form of a meditation, a journaling session, a gratitude exercise, or a walk outside. When you give children time to think back on their day in a nonjudgmental way, they can see what they have accomplished and what actions they need to take to keep moving forward.

Gratitude

Gratitude is thankful appreciation for what we have received, both tangible and not. A young child might be grateful for a visit from abuela and abuelo, a loving family pet, or a trip to the strawberry farm. Gratitude makes people focus on what they have—not what they lack. It is found in all cultures.

Gratitude is strongly and consistently associated with optimism and greater happiness. Simply writing a letter to thank someone for her kindness does as much for the letter writer as it does for the recipient (Seligman 2006). Gratitude helps people feel positive emotions more often, relish good experiences, improve their health, deal with adversity, and build strong relationships.

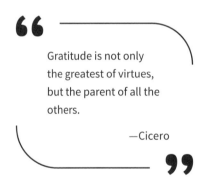

> Gratitude is not only the greatest of virtues, but the parent of all the others.
>
> —Cicero

Consider the many ways you can enhance children's gratitude, by encouraging them with the following activities (Harvard Medical School 2011):

- **Write a thank-you note.** Have each child write a thank-you note to someone she values. The recipient might be a family member, a former teacher, their bus driver, someone met on a field trip, or anyone else the child appreciates. Children can dictate while you write their words. They can then make drawings to go with their notes. At the end, help deliver their notes by walking together to mail the letters or by emailing them together from a computer, smartphone, or tablet.

- **Thank someone mentally.** No time to write a thank-you on a particular day? Just thinking about someone who has done something nice is helpful. Encourage children to mentally thank these individuals.
- **Keep gratitude journals.** Make writing in gratitude journals a part of your daily routine. Children can draw something they are grateful for while you write in your journal about something you appreciated. Share entries with the children at group times.
- **Count blessings.** Pick a time every week to sit down and talk about your good fortunes in life. Encourage the children to think back on what has gone well and what they are grateful for. Have them reflect on the sensations they feel when something good happens.
- **Meditate.** Mindfulness meditation involves focusing on the present moment without judgment. Encourage children to concentrate on what they're grateful for.

Happiness is not something ready-made. It comes from your own actions.

—Dalai Lama

Happiness

In the United States, the pursuit of happiness is a constitutional right—along with life and liberty. Happy people experience joy, contentment, and positive well-being. They have a sense that life is good, meaningful, and worthwhile (Lyubomirsky 2008). This definition captures both the fleeting positive emotions that come with an immediate sense of happiness as well as the deeper, long-term sense of meaning and purpose.

Happy people reap many benefits.

- They have stronger immune systems than unhappy people.
- They live longer, increasing their lifespan by seven and a half to ten years.
- They handle stress better and recover faster from trauma.
- They maintain better relationships, including marriage.
- They are more philanthropic.

Happy and unhappy people generally encounter the same number of adverse events in their lives. But optimists are willing and able to interpret adverse events positively, leading to long-term happiness. Pessimistic people, on the other hand, focus on negativity and experience unhappiness. To be authentically happy, one needs to be optimistic.

Use the following strategies to teach young children how to enhance happiness (Lyubomirsky 2008):

- **Count your blessings together.** Draw children's attention to events that are happy. "Good news: next week we are going on a field trip to the zoo!"

- **Encourage acts of kindness.** Comment when you observe a child doing something nice for another person. "I saw you invite Ramon to help you in the garden. He was sitting alone under the tree. I saw him smiling while you worked together."

- **Value friends and friendships.** Talk with children about what it means to be a friend and how friends make each other happy. "That was great that you helped Norah clean up the mess after she knocked the paint containers over. Having your help made her feel a lot better. You were a good friend to her, like she is to you."

- **Make it possible to do more things children enjoy doing.** Help all children recognize the things they enjoy, and make them part of your program. "Let's walk to the park when we go outdoors—I know Hannah and Rita have been eager to collect leaves!"

- **Recall enjoyable people and experiences.** Ask questions that help children reflect on treasured past events. "Do you remember how happy you were when…?"

- **Learn to forgive.** Be a role model for forgiveness, and comment when you see a child forgiving others. "You and Trixie were upset with each other. I'm glad you put your differences aside."

- **Encourage healthy habits.** Ensure that your program offers nutritious meals and snacks, provides sufficient nap/rest time, and encourages fitness. When children are well fed, rested, and healthy, they can concentrate on making choices that will bring them happiness. "We have pears and peaches for afternoon snack. Help yourself when you feel hungry."

Kindness

Kindness is the quality of being warmhearted, considerate, humane, and sympathetic. An act of kindness is a spontaneous gesture of goodwill toward someone or something—be it a child, an adult, an animal, or nature. Kindness is valued by most societies and religions. For free societies to function, citizens need to look beyond narrow self-interest and consider the public good.

Preschool and kindergarten are particularly good times to teach children about kindness. Between the ages of four and seven, the brain is especially receptive to learning and developing lifelong, positive emotional habits. According to a 2017 survey by Sesame Street Workshop, 78 percent of teachers and 73

Kindness is a language which the deaf can hear and the blind can see.

—Mark Twain

percent of parents believe that kindness is essential for future success, even more so than good grades.

For educators seeking to bring kindness into their programs, the Center for Healthy Minds at the University of Wisconsin–Madison has developed a Kindness Curriculum for preschoolers. It is being used in more than fifteen thousand classrooms worldwide. Likewise, the Random Acts of Kindness Foundation has developed lesson plans for kindergarten and higher-grade teachers to introduce Kindness in the Classroom. Both of these resources are available free of charge to educators. See https://centerhealthyminds.org/join-the-movement/sign-up-to-receive-the-kindness-curriculum and www.randomactsofkindness.org/for-educators.

Optimism is an integral part of kindness. Both are linked to understanding emotions, self-regulation, and gratitude. Being kind to oneself is basic to both kindness and optimism. Imagine a child having difficulty writing his name. If he thinks to himself, "I'm stupid. I can't do anything right," then he's being both pessimistic and unkind to himself. In contrast, if he can reframe his thoughts and say to himself, "I wrote the E correctly. I just have more letters to learn," then he's being both optimistic and kind to himself.

Here are some ways young children can express kindness (Sheakoski 2015). They can do some of these tasks on their own, and some with your assistance.

- Hold the door open for someone.
- Collect litter.
- Let someone go ahead of them in line.
- Compliment a friend's efforts.
- Tell someone why they are special.
- Make someone new at school feel welcome.
- Invite someone to play.
- Share a special toy with a friend.
- Teach someone something new.
- Make a homemade gift for someone.
- Smile at everybody—it's contagious.

There is great overlap among the practices of resilience, mindfulness, growth mindset, grit, gratitude, happiness, and kindness. Optimism is a key component of each of these practices and their development. Children who are resilient, are mindful, have a growth mindset, develop grit, practice gratitude, are authentically happy, and act with kindness will also be optimistic.

Next, we will explore strategies you can use to make optimism an ongoing part of young children's education.

CHAPTER 2

Explanatory Style: How Optimism Is Learned

The optimist sees the donut, the pessimist sees the hole.

—OSCAR WILDE

For educators the main takeaway from the research on optimism is that optimism can be learned and practiced. Even though there is a genetic component to optimism, it is not a fixed trait, such as eye color. It is a way of looking at life's events and explaining them to oneself.

As human beings, we interpret life through the lens of what psychologists call an *explanatory style*. This determines whether we see an opportunity to make lemonade or a basket of sour lemons. However, the good news is that we can make a conscious effort to develop an explanatory style that promotes optimistic thought and diminishes pessimistic thought. We can even rewire our brains to think more optimistically.

Since a wealth of research studies have concluded that optimism makes us healthier, happier, and more successful in both school and life, it behooves us all to become more optimistic. And what greater gift can we give children than to help them lay the groundwork for a lifetime of optimism?

History of Learned Optimism

The origins of learned optimism can be traced back to experiments conducted by Martin Seligman and his colleagues during the 1960s and '70s. As you read about these experiments, remember that they occurred in another era—when the use of electric shocks with animals was considered an appropriate research technique.

As a young grad student in experimental psychology, Seligman conducted an experiment on classical conditioning of dogs. He and his colleagues would ring a bell and then lightly shock the dogs. After repeating this several times, the dogs would react merely to the sound of the bell and act as if they had been shocked. Instead of being conditioned to eat at the sound of a bell, as Pavlov's dogs were, Seligman's dogs were conditioned to expect to be shocked.

Something unexpected, though, happened when Seligman put these conditioned dogs into a shuttlebox for a second experiment. A shuttlebox is a cage divided into two halves by a low hurdle. The floor of one side was wired to provide light shocks, and the other side was not.

Seligman predicted that if the experimenters rang a bell, the dogs would hop over the hurdle to escape the shock they knew was coming. But most of these dogs didn't do as expected. They stayed where they were and endured the shock.

The behavior of these conditioned dogs was in stark contrast to "naive" dogs who had not participated in any previous experiments. The naive dogs jumped the hurdle to avoid being shocked, as expected.

Why the difference in behavior between these groups? The dogs from the earlier experiment had been conditioned to expect shocks; they had simply given up trying. Having learned they were helpless in the previous situation, they continued being helpless in this new experiment—even though they could have readily changed their circumstances. They experienced what Seligman termed "learned helplessness."

Donald S. Hiroto, a graduate student at Oregon State University, replicated Seligman's dog experiments with humans in the early 1970s. In his studies, he exposed human subjects to noise rather than electric shocks.

In the initial conditioning experiment, one group of college students was exposed to a loud noise that could be stopped by pressing a button. A second group had their hands secured so they couldn't move them to press the button that would stop the noise. A designated third group did not participate in this first phase of the experiment.

Hiroto then had these same three groups participate in a second experiment in which they were again exposed to loud noise. This time they could turn off the noise by moving their fingers from one side of a box to another, in what could be considered a human shuttlebox.

As with Seligman's dogs, most of the students from the group that had been unable to move their hands in the first phase failed to do anything in this situation where they were in fact free to move their hands. And like the naive dogs, subjects in the other two groups quickly learned to turn off the noise.

Whether canine or human, learned helplessness occurs when we aren't in control of our destiny. If we believe there is nothing we can do to change a bad situation, we simply give up. To everyone's surprise, though, not all subjects experienced learned helplessness. In both the canine and human experiments, approximately one-third of the subjects did not succumb to learned helplessness. Although this subgroup had been exposed to situations where nothing they did made a difference, the experimenters could not make these plucky subjects remain helpless in future situations.

Seligman was captivated by these anomalies. What made these canine and human subjects keep going in the face of seemingly helpless and hopeless situations? Why did they persevere? This is how Seligman summarized his realization:

> Who gives up easily and who never gives up? Who survives when his work comes to nothing or when he is rejected by someone he has loved long and deeply? And *why*? Clearly, some people don't prevail: like helpless dogs, they crumple up. And some do prevail; like the indomitable experimental subjects, they pick themselves up and…manage to go on and rebuild.…
>
> Now, after seven years of experiments, it was clear to us that the remarkable attribute of resilience in the face of defeat need not remain a mystery. It was not an inborn trait: it could be acquired. (2006, 30)

Seligman thus turned his attention from what makes us helpless to what makes us hopeful. Who are these optimists who refuse to give up in the face of adversity? What is it that they know and do? And how can we teach others to embrace this same spirit of resilience and learn to flourish?

It All Comes Down to Our Explanatory Style

What Seligman and his colleagues found is that people who don't become helpless in the face of adversity look at events differently than those who succumb to helplessness. Resilient people interpret events in ways that lead them to optimistic behaviors and actions. In contrast, helpless people interpret events in ways that lead them to pessimistic behaviors and actions. Seligman termed this interpretive practice an *explanatory style*.

An explanatory style can be thought of as the stories people use to explain the cause of any event—good or bad. These self-explanations predispose us to feel either pessimistic or optimistic. Our explanatory style thus becomes the prism through which we experience life either helplessly or hopefully.

As Seligman further notes, there are three dimensions people use to explain why any event happens: permanence, pervasiveness, and personalization. Often designated as the "Three Ps," these perceptions steer us toward optimism or pessimism, as described below.

Permanence: "How Long Will the Situation Last?"

Pessimists see adversity as permanent, all-reaching, and everlasting. In contrast, they view good fortune as a short-lived, temporary event.

- A pessimistic adult might think, "I don't know why I try diets, they never work."
- A pessimistic child might think, "Sterling doesn't want to play with me. No one is ever going to want to play with me."

Optimists see adversity as a temporary setback caused by a passing misfortune. They tend to see good fortune, on the other hand, as long lasting.

- An optimistic adult might think, "I broke my diet tonight, but I'm going to stay with it. I'll stock up on nutritious foods so I'm not tempted to go out to eat."
- An optimistic child might think, "Sterling didn't want to play blocks with me, but I bet he'll want to play outdoors with me."

The difference: Optimists see bad events as passing; pessimists see them as ongoing. Conversely, optimists see good events as permanent; pessimists see them as transient.

Pervasiveness: "How Much of My Life Will This Situation Affect?"

Pessimists tend to think that when problems arise, everything is ruined. On the other hand, they find the effects of good fortune to be greatly limited.

- A pessimistic adult might tell herself, "My bus was late again today. My program director is going to fire me."
- A pessimistic child might think to himself, "I can't finish this puzzle. I'm too dumb to do anything."

Optimists see the effects of a bad situation as limited. In contrast, they see the effects of good events as far-reaching.

- An optimistic adult might think, "I'm only ten minutes late. I'm sure my assistant got everyone together for morning meeting. I'll talk with my director before she comes to me, and I'll tell her I'll start taking the earlier bus from now on."
- An optimistic child might think, "This is a really hard puzzle. It must be for big kids. Next time I'll try one I know I can do."

The difference: Optimists see problems as being specific to occasions or circumstances. Pessimists see unhappy events as being universal and affecting everything in their lives. On the other hand, optimists see good events as all-encompassing, while pessimists see them as having limited repercussions.

Personalization: "Who or What Caused the Situation?"

Pessimists tend to think they cause adverse events, even when logically that makes no sense. When something goes well, though, they believe it is because of an outside event, not their own efforts.

- A pessimistic adult might think, "That certification exam sure was easy. They must not expect teachers to know very much. Otherwise I never would have passed."
- A pessimistic child might think, "Ava's birthday party was ruined because I got sick and had to leave early. Everyone's mad at me."

Optimists tend to think that when something goes well, it is because of their own efforts. When a problem occurs, however, they find reasons for the adversity outside of themselves. Note: Because optimism needs to be rooted in reality, there are times when an optimist may be responsible for the adverse situation. In these cases, the optimist still puts the situation in perspective and figures out how to turn around the problem.

- An optimistic adult might think, "All my hard work paid off. I easily passed the certification exam."
- An optimistic child might think, "I wish I hadn't gotten sick, but sometimes that just happens. At least we had lots of fun before I had to leave. And when I'm better, I'm going to invite Ava over to play with me."

The difference: Optimists externalize the causes of bad situations, while pessimists blame themselves. When good fortune occurs, optimists see themselves as having controlled the situation while pessimists believe their good fortune is due to outside circumstances or other people.

> **❝**
>
> In our class, we discussed the Three Ps with a focus on permanence, thus giving each child the vocabulary needed to understand optimism. We then used a Transformer analogy. (Transformers are robot toys that can change into vehicles.) We added the catchphrase "transform your thinking" to help children understand that they can change their perception of a situation.
>
> —Stacey Michalski, Teacher
>
> **❞**

Developing an Explanatory Style

We form our explanatory styles as young children. As explained in chapter 1, humans have a genetic predisposition toward an optimistic or pessimistic explanatory style. However, our environment, interactions, and life experiences impact how we interpret events and whether our explanatory styles will remain as they were at birth.

The seeds of explanatory style germinate during the first few years of life. The concepts of optimism and pessimism emerge at around ten months of age, following the development of object permanence, when babies understand that objects continue to exist when out of sight. Prior to this time, the idea of a positive or negative future cannot exist because a baby's perspective is focused on the present.

In the preschool years (what Jean Piaget terms the preoperational stage of development), children begin learning to think symbolically and can then start developing an explanatory style. While in this stage of rapid cognitive development, children play make-believe, take on pretend roles, dream, talk, and understand the concept of number. During these activities children might think in optimistic ("I can do so many things") or pessimistic ("I can't do anything right") terms.

As with all learned skills, explanatory styles form along a developmental continuum. Some children have more fully developed explanatory style skills than others. And as in all areas of development, children have their own timetables.

Children's explanatory styles remain fluid during preschool and kindergarten, which are times of ongoing development. As they rapidly grow, develop, learn, and experience the world, children begin to learn how to explain life to themselves.

Depending on their inborn tendencies as well as what they perceive and observe in their environment, children start explaining things either optimistically or pessimistically. In addition, exposure to the following three influences will likely impact how young children develop explanatory styles:

- the explanatory style of teachers, parents, and other important adults in their lives

- the feedback or criticism children receive from their trusted role models
- the experience of life-altering events

Family members and teachers are important role models in all aspects of children's lives. Therefore, the way teachers, parents, and other influential adults interpret life can shape how children interpret theirs. If children see parents or teachers interpreting problems as temporary, specific, and externally caused, then they will get the message that an optimistic outlook is the appropriate way to interpret these events.

For example, after a hurricane causes a flood in the classroom, Ms. Everheart, an optimistic preschool teacher, tells the children, "We'll be having class in the gym for a few weeks. We can make toys to play with, and soon we'll be back in our regular classroom."

Conversely, children learn pessimistic behaviors if they are modeled. There is a strong correlation between a parent's explanatory style (especially that of the mother) and the child's explanatory style (Peterson and Bossio 1991; Vélez et al. 2014).

To illustrate, when her husband loses his job, a pessimistic mother might say, "I don't know if Dad will ever get a new job. We must be careful about what we spend money on. Marta, this means we can't get you any new toys for your birthday."

Children's explanatory styles are also influenced by the feedback or criticism they receive from their trusted role models. If teachers and parents communicate that children's problems are temporary and limited, then children feel optimistic about the outcome.

An optimistic parent might say, "Marcus, I know peeling that carrot seemed hard, but remember, this was your very first time. Now that you know how to use the peeler, it will be easier next time."

The reverse is true of feedback that implies the problem is permanent and its effects are all-encompassing. "Marcus, you made a real mess of that carrot. From now on, I don't want you peeling carrots."

Lastly, the experience of life-altering events can impact how children develop their explanatory styles. Stressful realities and crises—the death of a parent, experiencing abuse or neglect, or long-term parental separation or divorce—can foster pessimism. Traumatic events can turn a child's world upside down in a minute's time. Thinking the worst-case scenario is permanent can become altogether too easy.

Similarly, though, overcoming challenges that feel overwhelming at the time can foster an optimistic explanatory style. Learning to ride a tricycle or being able to successfully write one's name can turn children's fears into confidence.

As children mature and have more experiences, their explanatory styles become more defined. By the time children are eight, their explanatory style is considered set. It will stay unchanged throughout the course of their lives unless there is an intentional intervention to help the child think optimistically, or unless the child chooses to modify her explanatory style as an adult. This is why it is so important to incorporate learned optimism into early childhood education programs. We want to teach all children to think optimistically and to have the adults who support and care for them think optimistically as well.

It Begins with ABC

How do educators help children change their explanatory style? The underlying strategy for fostering these changes has its roots in cognitive therapy. Developed by Aaron T. Beck and Albert Ellis in the 1960s, cognitive therapy is a short-term approach to treating anxiety, depression, and addiction. Rather than a long-term process of digging into childhood experiences, cognitive therapy focuses on changing current negative thinking—which has been learned. With a therapist's assistance, patients learn to examine, challenge, and unlearn their negative thinking and then focus on healthier alternatives. The brain becomes rewired for healthier living.

Cognitive therapy makes use of Ellis's ABC model, which helps explain our reactions to adversity. Ellis's underlying tenet is that adverse events do not cause us to behave in particular ways; rather, our *interpretation* of these events causes our behavior.

While developed for therapeutic use, the ABC model can be used in everyday life by both adults and children. It is expressed this way:

- **A** is for *adverse* event (what Ellis termed an activating event).
- **B** is for our *beliefs* and thoughts about the adverse event.
- **C** is for the *consequences* of having these thoughts and beliefs.

Let's apply the ABC model to a situation in an early childhood classroom. Ms. Hawkins tells five-year-old Omari, "The water table is so crowded, children are getting in one another's way. Since you've been there longer than everyone else, please finish up and choose another area to play in."

Some children might think nothing of this request, but Omari goes to a corner and starts to cry. Ms. Hawkins follows him and asks what is wrong.

"You were mean," he says. "You don't like me. Everybody's always picking on me."

It wasn't Ms. Hawkins' request that upset Omari; it was his interpretation of these events. Using the ABC model, this is what happened, according to Omari:

- **A** (Adversity): Ms. Hawkins asked me to stop a fun activity that others are still doing, and she told me to go somewhere else.

- **B** (Belief): I'm the only one who had to leave, so that must mean Ms. Hawkins doesn't like me as much as she likes the other children. That's why she picked me to leave.
- **C** (Consequences): I went to a corner of the room and cried.

As the teacher, Ms. Hawkins can use the ABC model to help Omari change his pessimistic interpretation of the situation by reexamining what happened and how he felt. *A* and *C* are usually easy to identify, but *B* is often unclear. In the example above, for instance, it is clear that being asked to leave the water table (*A*) caused a sad Omari to cry (*C*). But Omari may not understand the beliefs and feelings (*B*) that took him from *A* to *C*, especially while he is crying.

It's important, though, for children to understand their strong, sometimes debilitating emotions and beliefs. It is important too for adults to acknowledge these beliefs. Even if they appear irrational, beliefs are very real to the child. Children need to understand the cause of their feelings before they can do something about them.

Also keep in mind that while most adverse events (*A*) are obvious problems or unfortunate circumstances, there are times when they are seemingly happy events. In these cases, the child interprets a positive situation from a pessimistic perspective, turning it into an adverse event.

For example, perhaps Hashem looks at the ground, frowns, and purses his lips (*C*) when a classmate asks him to be her partner in setting the table for lunch (*A*). When you discuss the situation with Hashem, he tells you, "Andrea only picked me to be a helper because she knew you wanted her to and would be mad at her if she didn't." His pessimistic beliefs (*B*) turned this positive into a negative.

This is why it's important to help children understand the thoughts (*B*) shaping their behavior. Only when these thoughts and actions are acknowledged can something be done to recast them.

And Next Come D and E

Building on Ellis's ABC model, Martin Seligman and his colleagues developed a way to change anyone's negative explanatory style. This is where steps *D* and *E* come in:

- **D** is for *disputation* of the pessimistic beliefs.
- **E** is for the *energization* that is experienced when negative thoughts are successfully disputed.

These additional steps allow us to teach children (and ourselves) how to change a pessimistic explanatory style into an optimistic one. Disputation (*D*) involves looking for evidence that challenges the pessimistic beliefs (*B*). To do this, we coach children to look for alternative explanations and reactions to the adverse event (A).

Energization (E) is the result of challenging negative thoughts and building an optimistic approach. If E is repeated regularly in response to adverse reactions, over time the brain becomes reset for optimism.

Let's go back to the example with Omari to see how Ms. Hawkins can apply these additional steps to help him see the situation from a more optimistic perspective:

- **D** (Disputation): Ms. Hawkins disputes Omari's pessimistic beliefs (B) by explaining why she asked him to move. "I wasn't trying to be mean. There were too many children at the water table. Someone could get hurt. You were the first to arrive there, so I asked you to move on because other children had not had such a long turn." Ms. Hawkins also disputes Omari's interpretation that she doesn't like him. "I hope you know I like you a lot! At lunch today, I asked you to be a helper. Yesterday, after you fell off your trike, I cleaned the scrape and gave you a big hug. And last week at group time, I asked you to sit next to me and help take attendance. Can you think about how you felt at these times?"

- **E** (Energization): Having learned to see the event in a new light, Omari feels better about his relationship with Ms. Hawkins and why she asked him to leave the water table. He decides he doesn't mind leaving and is now ready to look at books in the library center.

As you talk with children and help them dispute (D) pessimistic thinking, use the Three Ps as a basis for generating alternative beliefs. With practice, many children will come up with their own strategies for overcoming difficult situations.

- **Permanence:** Help the child see that the setback or unhappy circumstance is temporary, that things can change. Suggest strategies a child can use to make the change: "You did drop a lot of food on the floor when you were eating, and I know that some of your friends were teasing you about it. Let's get the minivacuum and clean up the carpet right away. Starting at lunch tomorrow, I'll help you cut your food into smaller pieces. That way they'll be easier to eat and less likely to fall on the floor."

- **Pervasiveness:** Help the child see that the problem or unfortunate event has limited impact: "You're still learning to climb the monkey bars, and I know it's difficult. But that doesn't mean you're not already good at doing other things on the playground. You're very good at going down the slide and using the swings. Just this morning, I saw you and Linda throwing a ball together. If you'd like, I can help you practice climbing."

- **Personalization:** Help the child realistically process the event or problem. How the child feels about what happened—and why—makes all the difference. "It's not your fault that Snowball the hamster died, even though you were the last to take care of him. He was old and having trouble breathing. Remember how he wasn't even playing with his toys anymore?"

It is important for children to know they do not cause all negative situations and that not everything is their fault. However, if the child *did* cause the problem, it's equally important to help the child take responsibility rather than blame others. In these circumstances, the child needs to acknowledge facts while still focusing on turning the situation around: "It seems that you think Justin caused the fight because he didn't want to play with you. I know that it made you angry. But one of our classroom rules is that you can't hurt anyone. If you feel angry, you can find a teacher to talk with, go to the loft and hit the pillows, or use one of the toys from the calming basket. Later let's talk about some ways that you might invite Justin to play with you." (Before or after this discussion the teacher would also talk with Justin to find out his perspective on what happened. Perhaps Justin also needs to practice using his words to better express when he does not want to play with a classmate.)

Using the ABCDE Approach in an Early Childhood Setting

To teach children to think optimistically, the most important thing educators can do is make the ABCDE model an ongoing activity in the daily program. Every time a child reacts pessimistically to an adverse situation, pull the child to the side and have a private one-on-one discussion, as Ms. Hawkins did with Omari.

The following graphic depicts the development of explanatory style, as we react to both the challenges and good fortunes in life.

Here's how this might go in real life:

Teaching Optimism

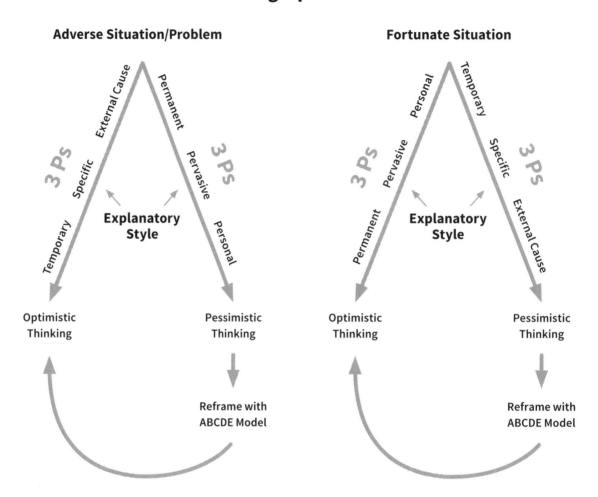

Ms. Cushing Helps Antonia Remember Her Friendships

Step A: Adversity

At morning meeting, Ms. Cushing reviews the gardening project the class started yesterday. "By now everyone should have planted something in our new outdoor garden. Do any of you still need to plant something?" she asks.

Antonia alone raises her hand. In a shaky voice, she says, "I wasn't here yesterday. Now there's no place left for me to plant!"

Step B: Beliefs

Seeing that Antonia is visibly upset, Ms. Cushing asks the assistant teacher to take over the group discussion. She gets up and sits next to Antonia so they can have a private conversation.

"Antonia, you look so sad," Ms. Cushing says softly. "Are you saying something to yourself that could be making you feel sad?"

"I always miss the good things," Antonia explains. "It's all my fault because I was gone! No one will want to let me plant now. I hate school! No one wants to be my friend!"

Step C: Consequences

Antonia bursts into tears, heaving and sighing as she cries.

Step D: Disputation

Ms. Cushing tries to calm Antonia. "Don't worry. It's not your fault you were absent yesterday while we were planting. There's still plenty of room for you to plant."

Antonia wipes her eyes but silently still heaves her shoulders.

Ms. Cushing gently challenges Antonia's explanatory style. "It's true you were the only one who missed out on planting, but that doesn't mean you 'always' miss out on things. Remember, just last week you went on the field trip to the bakery. And before that, you were here when Mr. Carlson brought musical instruments for us to play. We have photo albums in the library area with pictures of you at the bakery and playing the drums. I think you've been here for lots of fun things. Do you think that's true, Antonia?"

She nods.

"I bet there are children who will want you to put a plant near theirs. I know you have several good friends. Don't you and Tyler like to go down the slide together almost every day?"

Antonia nods again.

"And just the other day, I saw Jude bring you your painting to put in your cubby. Do you remember that?"

She nods once again.

"I'll bet either Tyler or Jude would like to garden together with you. Shall we go ask?"

Step E: Energization

Antonia perks up a bit. "Jude's my friend," she says. "Can I garden with him?"

Ms. Cushing smiles and replies, "Let's go ask him now."

To assist Antonia in changing her explanatory style from a pessimistic to an optimistic one, Ms. Cushing accepts the feelings Antonia expressed (*B*), but then works with her to gently dispute (*D*) those conclusions. One by one, she offers alternate conclusions for Antonia to consider, focusing on the Three Ps:

- **Permanence:** How long will the troublesome situation last? Antonia believes bad things "always" happen to her. This pessimistic view exaggerates the permanence of the event. Her teacher offers a more optimistic view, explaining that this was a one-time unhappy event. She wants Antonia to see that she doesn't always miss out on the fun and won't necessarily miss out on anything in the future.
- **Pervasiveness:** How much of my life will it affect? How far-reaching is it? Pessimists tend to think, "Now everything is ruined!" Antonia mentally leaps from missing one event to hating school. Optimists, on the other hand, believe that the effects of an adverse situation are limited. Ms. Cushing helps Antonia make a more accurate assessment of the situation by being specific about what has happened. She also focuses on what her next steps might be to improve the situation.
- **Personalization:** Who is responsible? Who or what caused the situation? Pessimists tend to think they cause adverse events, even when it's obvious that they didn't. Antonia thinks she's to blame by being absent the day before. She is afraid her classmates are mad at her and won't let her put her plant near theirs. She deals with her fear by concluding that she has no friends. Her teacher reassures her it was not her fault that the situation occurred. Ms. Cushing also explains that Antonia does indeed have friends, citing examples of times she and other children happily played together.

By helping Antonia view the Three Ps in a different light, Ms. Cushing helps Antonia reach an optimistic conclusion, where she can join her peers in planting a garden.

After going through steps *A*, *B*, *C*, and *D*, Antonia asks her friend Jude if they can garden together. An energized (*E*) and more optimistic Antonia has a new perspective on the activity. More importantly, she has a new perspective on how she fits into the classroom and is viewed by others.

It's important to remember that as successful as it was, a conversation like Ms. Cushing had with Antonia is not a one-time fix. The teacher will need to have a number of conversations such as this so that eventually Antonia will be able to dispute her own pessimistic thinking. Using the ABCDE process repeatedly and regularly will help children like Antonia develop an optimistic explanatory style.

I am grateful that we opened up the topic and started teaching the children about optimism. At first the children gave me a clueless look: "Huh?!" Weeks later they understood the importance of finding the positive in different situations.

Through implementation of positive talk and using their words, playtime has less tears, less arguing, and more sharing. We now hear, "When you are done playing with that, can I play with it?" and "I really wanted to play with magnetic tiles, but I'll play with blocks and animals."

—Danielle Cooper, Lead Pre-K Teacher

Overcoming Obstacles to the ABCDE Process

Sometimes it is difficult for very young children to figure out what exactly is bothering them—step *B* in the ABCDE process. You may ask them, "What's wrong?" and get an unhelpful answer, such as "Nothing," or a response that's unrelated to the actual situation.

To help children get to the root of the problem and express their beliefs out loud, try phrasing your questions in ways such as these:

- "What are you saying to yourself?"
- "What are you thinking inside your head?"
- "What is your head telling you?"

Research has shown that when asked to reflect on what their head is telling them, young children can grasp what they are thinking and feeling (Hall and Pearson 2004). Thus they are better able to convey these thoughts and feelings to others—as well as to themselves.

Asking, "What is your head saying to you?" (or a variation thereof) has been the most effective change. Previously I would say, "What should you do?" and so on. The children had a lot of canned answers: "I should be listening," "sitting," "sharing." When I switched to "What is your head telling you?" the children gave answers like "I'm angry" or "I should wait my turn." This led to more significant interactions and discussions with the children.

—Alicia Weeber, Pre-K Teacher

As you use the ABCDE model, also keep in mind that to help children change their thinking styles, you have to help them overcome typical "thinking traps." These thinking traps are due to the human tendency to simplify the information we process and take mental shortcuts.

We do this because humans take in more information through our senses than we can ever process. Unconsciously and automatically, we tend to process only information that supports our beliefs, while filtering out information that goes against our currently held beliefs. Known as *confirmation bias*, this tendency causes us to draw conclusions based on limited information. If we are honest with ourselves, we can see this in action when we read or watch TV. We soak in information that confirms what we already believe, and we tend to eschew the opposing viewpoint.

Thinking traps go against the accurate and flexible thinking that is the foundation of an optimistic explanatory style. Therefore, when it comes to working with children, we need to be alert to these thinking traps and help children overcome them. In *The Resilience Factor* (2002), Reivich and Shatté identify several common thinking traps:

1. **Jumping to conclusions:** making an assumption about a person or event based on little or no factual data. Example: Talia sees Julie sorting the leaves from the morning nature walk. Talia goes to the table where Julie is working. She assumes that since Julie is her friend, there's an open invitation to join her. But when Julie asks Betsy to join her instead, Talia is crushed.

2. **Mind reading:** assuming we know what others are thinking or assuming others can guess what we are thinking without being told. Example: At lunchtime, Peyton can't decide where he should sit. He wants to go to the table Junior is sitting at but says to himself, "I just know that Junior won't want to eat lunch with me."

3. **Emotional reasoning:** drawing a conclusion based on feelings or intuition rather than fact. Example: Staring at the new climbing apparatus on the playground, Jeremy says to himself, "I should be able to climb up high like Daphne, but I don't think I can. I'm not going to even try."

4. **Overgeneralizing:** making sweeping judgments about people or events based on limited experience. Example: After the teacher suggests that Sharon and Amanda try weaving fabric into the fence outdoors, Sharon immediately gets the hang of it. Amanda, however, tries twice but is unsuccessful. She throws all the scarves on the ground and thinks, "I can't do anything right."

5. **Magnifying/minimizing:** over- or underemphasizing certain aspects of a situation; making mountains out of molehills or exaggerating importance. Example: James laughed and played with several friends during the day. Yet when his dad came to pick him up, James said, "My day was terrible. Marco only wanted to play with Zach."

6. **Catastrophizing:** assuming the worst-case scenario is in place. Example: Bobby accidentally knocks the basket of collage materials on the floor. He thinks, "The teacher is going to be really mad at me. I'll never get to make things again. I bet I can't even play in the art center ever again."

As shown in the above examples, thinking traps can lead to pessimistic thinking. It's important for educators to gently challenge children's negative thoughts and help them interpret events more positively. By using accurate and flexible thinking, teachers can lead children toward realistic optimism.

Implementing the ABCDE Model

As already established, it takes more than a one-time conversation—such as the one Ms. Hawkins had with Omari or Ms. Cushing had with Antonia—to change a child's explanatory style. But using the ABCDE process repeatedly and regularly will indeed help children develop a positive explanatory style. When you incorporate these types of conversations into your regular programming, children can become aware of their feelings and reframe their negative thoughts into optimistic thinking. Ultimately they will use the model themselves and become optimistic thinkers.

Real-life classroom events can serve as effective conversation starters. You can use the ABCDE process whenever you see a child facing an adverse event— whether she's frustrated with a challenging puzzle, struggling to learn the lyrics of a song, having a hard time making friends, or finding it difficult to stand in line for transitions. Whenever an adverse event (A) leads to pessimistic thinking and behavior (B) and an unhappy consequence (C), you can work one-on-one with the affected child to help dispute and reinterpret (D) her thinking and show her a more optimistic, energized outcome (E).

Keep in mind that there is no set timetable for using the ABCDE strategy. How children interpret daily classroom events will dictate when and how often you need to have one-on-one conversations. Eventually you want children to be able to independently dispute their own negative thinking and generate alternative explanations for events. For some children in your class, this will be a straightforward process. For others it may be a long road.

We do know, though, that the more often and the more effectively you use the ABCDE process, the more likely all the children in your class will become optimistic thinkers. Realistic, healthy optimism is the end goal of using the ABCDE process. Karen Reivich (2008), one of the pioneers in the field of using learned optimism with young children, puts it this way: "Realistic optimism keeps you shooting for the stars without losing sight of the ground below."

Why We Know This Works

Research shows that the ABCDE model turns pessimistic thought into optimistic thinking, and that it can rewire the brain for optimism if done repeatedly and regularly. There are two strong examples of this life-changing process at work with children.

First, Seligman and his students at the University of Pennsylvania created and ran the Penn Resiliency Program (PRP) from 1990 to 2007. PRP worked with teachers in the United States, Australia, and the United Kingdom to teach school-age children how to identify pessimistic explanations and to generate more optimistic and realistic explanations for problems they encountered.

PRP's successes have been validated in some twenty controlled research studies involving thousands of children. Evaluation results consistently show significant results. Notably the PRP children who changed their explanatory styles the most were those who had been the most pessimistic and at the greatest risk for depression at the start of the program. And based on follow-up studies, these results were long lasting.

While PRP focused on school-age children, a resilience program known as Reaching IN... Reaching OUT (RIRO) adapted the PRP model for children ages two to eight. RIRO is an ongoing teacher- and parent-training program initiated in 2002 by the Child & Family Partnership in Ontario, Canada.

Through RIRO, adults who work with young children learn to model thinking and coping strategies that will help children develop optimistic explanatory styles. RIRO also helps children learn to "reach in" (think more flexibly and accurately) and "reach out" (take on new opportunities).

Evaluations of the pilot and five additional phases of the program document positive changes in children's explanatory styles. In addition, the pilot study (Hall and Pearson 2004) showed these related benefits as well:

- 100 percent of participating teachers reported the program having a positive impact on children's behavior. No statistical differences were reported between children in preschool and kindergarten.
- 65 percent of teachers reported improvements in children's impulse control (executive function).
- 61 percent of teachers reported improvements in emotional regulation.
- 86 percent of teachers said the program positively affected their interactions with other adults, including colleagues (82 percent).
- Teachers reported that the most important skills taught by the program included the following:
  1. Putting adversities and challenges into perspective

2. Calming and focusing oneself
3. Using the ABC[DE] model to understand how their own beliefs about the causes and consequences of adversity affect the response

The Canadian RIRO program is especially important in that it has shown that children as young as preschool age are developmentally capable of thinking about their thinking—the skill of metacognition. While not every young child is able to do this in depth, most preschoolers can tell you what they are thinking in their heads. This means that they have the ability to discuss steps *B* and *D* of the learned optimism process. Here's how the evaluators of the RIRO Pilot Program Evaluation described it:

> Teachers expressed some surprise at how much young children could tell them about their thinking if they were simply asked. They were excited to report that they had formulated age-appropriate questions to help children express their thought processes and beliefs, such as, "What are you saying to yourself?" and "What are you thinking in your head?" Teachers talked about the impact on their practice of asking about children's thoughts and beliefs, in addition to inquiring about their feelings, when adversities and stresses occurred. The PRP [Penn Resiliency Project] model added a whole new layer to their practice with children. This expanded focus has major implications for professionals' and paraprofessionals' observations, assessments, and interventions with young children. (Hall and Pearson 2004, 9)

By harnessing young children's ability to understand their feelings and think about adversity, adults can gently lead children in turning negative thoughts into positive ones. And by using the ABCDE steps, we can help young children learn to think optimistically, thus building a foundation for a lifelong use of an optimistic explanatory style. This one activity alone can make a major difference in children's school and life success.

Next we will explore how you can create a classroom atmosphere to support the use of the ABCDE model and implement other strategies that lead children to develop or enhance optimistic-thinking skills.

CHAPTER 3

Creating a Climate for Teaching Optimism

Teaching is the greatest act of optimism.

—Colleen Wilcox

Teaching optimism cannot be done in a vacuum. To help children change their explanatory styles, you have to first create a program that will support and re-inforce this practice. Through your program's philosophy and physical setup, you create a climate that reflects and enhances the content you teach. In this chapter, we describe the elements of such an early childhood setting and suggest strategies that lay a foundation for the effective teaching of optimism.

Curricular Skills That Support Teaching Optimism

In setting up your program to support children's development of optimism, you need to consider what you want your program to accomplish. What philosophy and educational practices will enhance children's learning of optimism? Your first consideration, therefore, should be to review your program's mission statement, goals, and curriculum to see how well they support the teaching of optimism. Should you find they are not supportive of optimism or only mildly supportive, you'll need to refine them to align with the information presented in this chapter.

From the research literature (Peterson and Bossio 1991; Seligman 2007; Reivich and Shatté 2002; Reivich 2008; Hewitt and Heidemann 1998), we have identi-fied nine skills to include in your program that will enhance teaching and learning about optimism. To become optimistic thinkers, children will benefit from learn-ing how to identify and regulate emotions, use executive functions, possess confi-dence and self-efficacy, be independent, take risks, persevere, solve problems, be empathic, and self-calm. If you address each of these skills in your program's cur-riculum, you will predispose children to learning how to think optimistically.

Identify and Regulate Emotions

The difference between optimists and pessimists is not in the emotions they have but in the way they interpret, express, address, and are affected by their emotions. While pessimists tend to get caught up in negative emotions and feel paralyzed by them, optimists can cope with their feelings and move forward. Optimism is the opposite of helplessness. An optimist will not be stymied by negative emotions or feelings.

Teaching young children to be optimistic thinkers begins with helping them identify and name their emotions—both negative and positive—so that they are aware of what they are experiencing. As *New York Times* columnist Tony Schwartz (2015) writes, "Naming our emotions tends to diffuse their charge and lessen the burden they create."

The next step for educators is to help children examine the cause(s) of their negative emotions so they can learn to regulate them. Teachers can then work with children in learning how to respond to the initial problem in a more positive way. This is a foundational skill in learning how to think optimistically, as reflected in the ABCDE process described in chapter 2.

Let's see how this might play out in the classroom setting.

But feelings can't be ignored, no matter how unjust or ungrateful they seem.

—Anne Frank

Mr. Doug Helps Sophie Address Her Negative Emotions

Five-year-old Sophie loves creating artwork on the computer, then printing and framing it. During morning choice time, she hurries to the computer in the art center, but she can't locate the drawing program she wants to use. She keeps searching, and when she can't find it, she throws the mouse in the air. Next she swats her chair so hard that it falls on the floor. That's when Mr. Doug comes over to help.

MR. DOUG: Sophie, please sit down and try to calm yourself. Take some deep breaths until you feel calmer. Let your angry feelings go.

SOPHIE: *(Takes deep breaths.)*

MR. DOUG: That's better. Your face doesn't look angry anymore. Can you tell me what's wrong, please? Look inside yourself and tell me what you're feeling.

SOPHIE: I'm angry. It's not fair. My program for making pictures is not there, and I want to use it.

MR. DOUG: I understand how that would make you frustrated. I know how much you enjoy the drawing program. I'll have to check into what's happening. But even though your favorite program's not there, it's not okay to throw things in our classroom.

Sophie: But I was mad.

Mr. Doug: It's okay to be angry when things don't go right. It's not okay, though, to throw things that might hurt others or could get broken. What might be a better choice than throwing things when you're upset?

Sophie: I guess I could not be mad.

Mr. Doug: That's an interesting thought, Sophie. But all of us get mad at times. And it's okay to feel that way. Perhaps next time you could try to talk with me if you get upset. And if you feel like you just have to throw things, you could go to the calm-down corner and throw beanbags into a basket. Do you still feel like throwing things?

Sophie: I feel a little better. But I still want to throw things.

Mr. Doug: Okay. You can throw beanbags into a basket until you let go of all your angry feelings. Later I'll find out what happened to the drawing program. If there's a problem, I can reload it. Then you'll be able to make all the drawings you want.

Use Executive Functions

Executive functions refer to several mental skills that help us organize and act on information. These include focusing one's attention and remembering instructions. Executive function is also an extension of learning to control one's emotions. It is the difference between what we feel like doing and what we actually do—impulse control. According to Walter Gilliam, director of the Edward Zigler Center in Child Development and Social Policy at Yale's Child Study Center, "Executive function is the brain wrestling with its emotions.… Do I want to follow my first instinct or do I want to create a strategy that might work better? For young children, sometimes that means using their words, or getting the help of an adult, or realizing there's another toy they'd be happy playing with" (Larsen, accessed 2018).

Executive function skills directly support the development of optimistic thinking. A child who can plan, set goals, focus his attention, and think flexibly can use these skills to form an optimistic resolution to adversity (step E in the ABCDE process).

Being able to control impulses is likewise a vital skill in becoming optimistic. While it's not necessary or possible to eliminate impulses, it is very

If you look at what predicts how well children will do later in school, more and more evidence is showing that executive functions—working memory and inhibition—actually predict success better than IQ tests.

—Adele Diamond

important to hold them in check. To think optimistically, children need to internalize a "stop and think" mechanism that will allow them to make healthy actions and choices.

Here are some strategies teachers can use to promote this skill:

- **Encourage high-level sociodramatic play.** This type of play requires planning and focus. Children take on roles that follow rules agreed upon by all the players, and to stay involved in the play, they must inhibit actions that don't conform to those rules.
- **Read aloud with individual children.** Afterward ask the child to retell the story or act it out. This involves paying attention to characters, juggling plot points in working memory, and planning the sequence of events.
- **Ask children to tell you stories of their own invention.** To do this children must organize their ideas, plan out character development, sequence events, and hold the plot in their working memory.
- **Play song and dance games.** Children use their working memory to recall repetitive lyrics. Freeze dances and games like musical chairs inhibit action and make use of control. Singing and dancing to a rhythm further enhance memory, attention, and inhibitory control.
- **Play board games.** Games challenge children to follow rules, wait for a turn, pay attention, remember moves, and handle winning and losing with grace.
- **Cook with children.** Cooking lets children practice following recipe instructions. Additionally the chefs learn to delay gratification, as they must wait until foods are prepared before eating them.

Possess Confidence and Self-Efficacy

The concept of self-efficacy refers to having faith in one's ability to succeed in the world, to solve life's problems and forge ahead. It involves defining goals and persevering to achieve them. Children with high self-efficacy are committed to solving problems and will persist until they succeed. Solving these problems gives them confidence, which spurs them to continue when they encounter the next problem.

Children with high self-efficacy and confidence approach challenges with determination, and they focus on what can go right, not what can go wrong—the hallmark of optimism. If one choice fails, they keep trying to resolve problems with conviction and a can-do attitude. They know their strengths and rely on them to make progress and eventually succeed.

> If I have the belief that I can do it, I shall surely acquire the capacity to do it even if I may not have it at the beginning.
>
> —Mahatma Gandhi

According to researchers Karen Reivich and Andrew Shatté (2002, 41), optimism and self-efficacy are connected to each other's development:

> Our research shows that optimism and self-efficacy often go hand in hand. Optimism is a boon if it is linked with true self-efficacy because optimism motivates you to search for solutions and to keep working hard to improve your situation.... The key to resilience and success...is to have realistic optimism coupled with self-efficacy.

The train in the childhood classic *The Little Engine That Could* has an optimistic view of his abilities. Reivich (2010) recommends that teachers use the following strategies to help children gain a similar sense of "I think I can!" competence:

- **Challenge negative thoughts.** The ABCDE model promotes optimism and also builds self-efficacy. For example, a child might tell her teacher that her mobile doesn't move because she "did not make it right." The teacher can help the child replace this negative thought with a truthful, positive one: "You did a fine job on your mobile. But it's not moving right now because we turned off the fan. There is no circulating air to move the mobile."

- **Teach goal setting.** Showing children how to break down their goals into interim steps can help build confidence and motivation toward reaching their end goal. Teaching children how to set realistic goals and strategies fosters successful outcomes.

- **Provide opportunities for mastery experiences.** Children need to try out ideas and see if their solutions meet stated goals. Mastery experiences give children both incentive to persevere and an environment that supports exploration and experimentation.

- **Notice, analyze, and celebrate successes.** Teachers can increase self-efficacy by teaching children to identify successes and to accurately assess their contributions. For example, when making a class mural, each artist can sign the portion of the mural he painted. Teachers can also photograph children's science experiments and post the photos with the scientists' names and their dictated descriptions of their process.

- **Offer process praise.** When teachers offer process praise, they notice and comment on children's efforts and the strategies they use to succeed. This type of praise helps create a growth mindset. It leads to greater mastery, persistence, and achievement than simply telling children they are "smart" or "good."

Be Independent

During the early years, children have an inborn drive to start doing things on their own. The words "me," "I can do it," and "mine" are heard first from toddlers and then repeatedly and insistently from preschoolers and kindergartners. One might think that unless there are physical or emotional impairments, most every child will naturally grow up to be independent.

> The spirit of independence in learning is one of the most valuable assets a learner can have, and we who want to help children's learning at home or in school must learn to respect and encourage it.
>
> —John Holt

This, however, is not always the case. In some environments and cultures, adults demonstrate their caring by doing things for children—including things children could likely do for themselves. They value dependence as a way to express love within the family and believe that learning to be independent can wait until the child is older. In addition, some parents and teachers value an "I'd rather do it for them" approach, because it takes time, effort, and patience to promote children's independence. In the short term, they find it is easier to put on a child's shoes than to wait for a child to do it herself.

Yet use of developmentally appropriate practice in early education settings encourages children to gain independence. It is fundamental to a number of cognitive and socioemotional skills that underpin child development in general and optimism in particular. Children who develop independence feel capable and powerful. This promotes optimistic thinking because independent children also feel in control of their future and expect positive outcomes. When teachers and educators take time to discuss this goal for children, they are likely to agree on an approach that balances cultural and family values with the program's curriculum and teaching approach.

Here are some of the many ways teachers can promote children's independence through the design of the classroom, program schedule, and choice of activities:

- Provide individual cubbies where children can store and retrieve their coats and possessions.
- Encourage children to put on and take off their own coats, other outerwear, shoes, and boots.
- Design learning centers with toys and materials displayed on low, open shelving labeled with pictures and words in all languages spoken by children in the class. Children can then take out, use, and return play materials on their own.
- Allow children to choose the learning center they wish to play in, what they want to do in that center, and how long they want to play there.
- Offer self-service snacks so children can get something healthy to eat when they are hungry.

- Provide dishes and utensils sized so children can serve themselves and eat independently.
- Provide child-size brooms, dustpans, mops, sponges, and trash cans so children can clean up after themselves.
- Offer tissues and paper towels on the tops of low shelves so children can wipe their own noses and hands.
- Post signs reminding children to wash their hands after certain activities and routines.
- Have individual toothbrushes and pump toothpaste so children can brush their teeth after eating.
- Involve children in taking out and replacing rest-time mats, cots, blankets, and lovies from home.

Take Risks

Risk taking involves both physical and cognitive actions. The ability to take risks, face potential setbacks, and keep on going is a forerunner to perseverance. If children fear failure and don't take risks, they limit what they can learn and accomplish. They may feel safe in doing the same things over and over, even though they have mastered them. Gaining new skills is difficult if a child won't leave his comfort zone and take on new challenges.

A ship is always safe at the shore—but that is *not* what it is built for.

—Albert Einstein

Teachers need to educate children about the value of failure. While it, of course, feels upsetting at the time, there is a positive flip side to failure. As has been demonstrated time after time, failure can pave the path to success. Positive psychologist Tal Ben-Shahar, whose course on happiness was the most popular offering in Harvard University's history, puts it this way:

> People who achieve great feats, no matter in what field, understand that failure is not a stumbling block but a stepping-stone on the road to success. There is no success without risk and failure. We often fail to see this truth because the outcome is more visible than the process—we see the final success and not the many failures that led to it. (2012, 130)

Many of us have heard the stories of artists, statesmen, and innovators who endured failure after failure before ever experiencing success. The president of Decca Records told Brian Epstein, the Beatles' manager, he was rejecting the Fab Four because "Guitar groups are on their way out" (Viner 2012). Colonel Sanders had his famous secret chicken recipe rejected 1,009 times before a restaurant finally accepted it. J. K. Rowling was rejected by twelve publishers before she finally found one to publish her Harry Potter stories. Beyoncé Knowles began singing as a child, but when her girl group failed to advance on *Star Search*, she was crushed.

It took eight years of hard work for her group to transform into Destiny's Child, which ultimately led her to stardom as Queen Bey. As these famous failures have shown us, we must "learn to fail or fail to learn" (Ben-Shahar 2012).

Early in life children need to learn that taking risks is the pathway to success. It is also the path to optimism. As Seligman sums it up, "In order for [a] child to experience mastery, it is necessary for him to fail, to feel bad, and to try again repeatedly until success occurs. None of these steps can be circumvented. Failure and feeling bad are necessary building blocks for ultimate success and feeling good" (2007, 44).

The following approaches will communicate the optimistic message that risking failure can be the gateway to success:

- **Offer empathy when a child is struggling or having a hard time.** Do not disregard the child's feelings or ask him to bury them. Acknowledge and respect the feelings by saying something such as, "I know you're disappointed, Carey. You wanted to write all the letters in your name the first time you tried."
- **Focus on the future.** Focus on actions that might improve the situation. "Justine, where might you place your plant so that it will have enough sunlight to grow?"
- **Reflect with the child on knowledge gained through the disappointment.** "Yancey, where do you think would be a better place to put your toothbrush so that no one accidentally knocks it over again?"
- **Offer a story or recollection about your own experiences.** Describe your failure and how you ultimately succeeded. "The first time I made bread, I didn't let the dough rise long enough. It came out like crackers! Now I use a timer."

Persevere

Those who persevere keep on trying and moving forward in the face of adversity and obstacles. It is a skill that all children and adults need if they are to survive and thrive in a world filled with challenges. Without perseverance, people give up when confronted by difficulties and experience helplessness.

Perseverance is a crucial component of optimism. Optimists make the conscious choice to keep trying when faced with adversity. One of the reasons children choose to persevere is because of the way they feel when they achieve goals. Whether they are learning to throw a ball into a hoop or zip a coat on their own, children experience a rush of positive emotions when they persevere and succeed: self-confidence, happiness, strength, and satisfaction. According to Barbara Frederickson (2001), these positive emotions help counteract negative feelings, promote creativity, and open children up to new possibilities. When perseverance becomes a habit, we feel empowered, which enhances our mental health, well-being, relationships, and community contributions—all examples of the benefits of optimism.

Here are some ways in which educators can encourage young children to persevere:

- **Involve children in setting their own behavioral and learning goals.** This allows them to know what they are working toward. Children are more likely to follow through if they have had a hand in establishing personal goals.
- **Start simple.** Help children identify the steps needed to reach their goals. Being able to complete an intermediate step or two offers children a sense of accomplishment and provides motivation to keep on going.
- **Teach children how to use tools related to the skills and tasks they are working on.** Activities such as woodworking, cooking, art, and music are much easier (and safer!) to accomplish when using the right tools. Children are more likely to succeed when they have the implements, guidance, and time they need to master a skill or complete a task.
- **Help children envision success.** With a mental image in mind, children become motivated to reach a goal. "What do you think it will feel like when you can create your own book for us to read?"
- **Applaud children's efforts, but avoid bribes and threats.** You can encourage perseverance by telling children you notice and celebrate their efforts. Threats and bribes, in contrast, work against perseverance.

> Perseverance has always just been something that was in me. And it was a tool that came in very handy as a ballerina.
>
> —Misty Copeland

Solve Problems

People who are optimistic thinkers can identify, address, and solve the problems that confront them. Every day brings a seemingly endless array of problems for children to solve: Damon won't share the dramatic play props, Janine's dad is late at pickup time, it's sleeting outside and we have to play indoors, one of the fish in the aquarium died, or the last two puzzle pieces are missing.

We know from the ABCDE approach that step A is identifying the adversity—that is, the problem. If teachers skip this step, they will likely stifle the child's burgeoning optimism. In steps D and E, children will come up with alternative interpretations for this adversity and then become energized to put these new interpretations into effect.

Educators can help children work through the model by teaching them the basic steps of problem solving:

1. Identify the problem.
2. Brainstorm some possible solutions. Target one that you think is most likely to work.
3. Imagine, "What will happen if I do this?"
4. Try the solution.
5. Evaluate whether the solution worked. If yes, that's great. If no, go back to step 2 and try another possible solution. Continue trying out possible solutions and evaluating them until the problem is successfully resolved.

Children who learn to solve problems feel confident and independent while simultaneously building optimism. Because problem solving is basic to learning, educators most likely have already targeted this skill as one they are helping children develop.

Here are some strategies for helping children develop problem-solving skills:

- **Pose open-ended questions.** During group meetings, ask questions that encourage the children to solve a problem. "Animals have been getting into our sandbox at night when no one is here. What can we do to keep the sandbox safe but not hurt any animals?"
- **Offer open-ended toys and materials.** Children can decide how to use these items on their own or with a friend.
- **Introduce new equipment, materials, and toys.** Share a new item at group time, then let children figure out what it does, how it works, and what to do with it.
- **Have the children act out problem solving.** They can do this through role-playing scenarios and puppet skits. For instance, a puppet doesn't want to share her toys with another puppet friend. The group discusses ways to help the puppets solve this problem.
- **Include problem solving as a part of activities.** Plan a scavenger hunt where children find clues by solving problems: "Find the next clue in the area where children go when they pretend to cook dinner."
- **Revisit problems that have been resolved.** How do children feel about the resolution in retrospect? Have the process and the solution helped make things better?

My optimism and confidence come not from feeling I'm luckier than other mortals, and they sure don't come from visualizing victory. They're the result of a lifetime spent visualizing defeat and figuring out how to prevent it.

—Chris Hadfield

Be Empathic

To have empathy is to understand, have compassion toward, and care about the feelings and circumstances of others. Researcher Brené Brown (accessed 2018) says that empathy consists of four qualities: the ability to take the perspective of another person, staying away from judgment, recognizing emotion in others, and communicating it. She notes that empathy is a "vulnerable choice" because it requires us to tap into something personal within ourselves in order to identify with the struggle of another.

When a good man is hurt all who would be called good must suffer with him.

—Euripides

Empathy is often confused with sympathy, but the terms are not interchangeable. Both are forms of concern for another person's well-being. Sympathy is an expression of care and concern and sometimes even pity. Empathy, however, involves experiencing others' feelings. According to Brown, it is the difference between feeling *for* (sympathy) and feeling *with* (empathy). Empathy is not just a response; it is a connection.

In preschool and kindergarten programs, we see empathy in action when a child hugs a crying classmate, offers to share a banana at snacktime with a hungry friend, or summons the teacher to help a peer who fell down. An empathic child feels sad for the penguin in a storybook who has lost his mommy and gives attention to a doll in the dramatic play area who is home alone.

Empathy is a complex process involving both cognitive and affective abilities. We must understand another person's perspective as well as care about how she feels. While empathy is not necessarily a part of optimism, they are best expressed in tandem. When the two are intertwined, the benefits of each are magnified. Bill Gates made a plea for this approach in the commencement address he and his wife, Melinda, gave at Stanford University in 2014:

> We want to make the strongest case we can for the power of optimism. Even in dire situations, optimism can fuel innovation and lead to new tools to eliminate suffering. But if you never really see the people who are suffering, your optimism can't help them. You will never change their world. . . . If we have optimism, but we don't have empathy—then it doesn't matter how much we master the secrets of science, we're not really solving problems; we're just working on puzzles. (Gates and Gates 2014)

Teachers can support children's development of empathy using these strategies:

- **Create an inclusive, diversity-embracing program.** This will help children recognize and understand commonalities and differences. Personal experiences with people from different backgrounds, cultures, and languages support children's appreciation for all. Even in homogeneous classrooms, teachers can introduce diversity through books, discussions, music, art, and other curricular areas. Research shows that teaching young children about multiculturalism promotes empathy—as well as happiness and school success (Dewar 2017).

- **Invite children to take on dramatic play roles of people very different from themselves.** Through play, children can learn to identify with varied experiences and perspectives. For example, challenge a child to play an elderly person, a pet dog, a child who uses a wheelchair, or an artist or musician.

- **Teach children to recognize and understand facial expressions.** Children can apply face-reading skills to better understand what a person is feeling. Read and discuss a picture book such as *The Way I Feel* by Janan Cain (2000) to help children learn how to look at facial expressions and figure out what another person is feeling.

- **Play charade-like small-group games.** Divide the group into two teams. One team will act out a person experiencing a particular emotion or feeling, while the other team observes and names that emotion or feeling. Switch roles so all have a turn acting and observing.

- **Offer a "do-over" so children can rethink their nonempathetic reactions.** In *UnSelfie: Why Empathetic Kids Succeed in Our All-About-Me World* (2016), Michele Borba suggests four steps to help a child enhance empathy with "CARE":
  ○ Call attention to uncaring behavior in private.
  ○ Assess how uncaring behaviors affect others, helping the child understand another's perspective.
  ○ Repair the hurt and make amends.
  ○ Express expectations for caring behavior in the future. Thus children learn how their actions affect others and eventually act empathetically without prompting.

- **Have one or more classroom pets.** Children can experience empathy as they care for and love the animal. Research from the Doris Day Animal Foundation (2004) shows that children who form a bond with their companion animals score higher on measures of empathy for both animals and humans. Children perceive pets as special friends and providers of social interactions, affection, and emotional support.

Self-Calm

Being able to calm oneself is an essential prerequisite to being able to think optimistically. Until children can recover from feeling upset, they cannot focus on anything else. Helping children learn how to self-calm enables them to think clearly. A calm child is able to concentrate on tasks and learning.

Self-calming is important for all children but particularly for those who have experienced trauma. For these children, it is not just everyday problems that trigger tears or anger but a constant fear of being unsafe.

Preschoolers and kindergartners are particularly receptive to building self-calming skills because they experience rapid brain growth in areas associated with self-regulation. This makes children responsive to and able to use self-calming techniques.

Teachers can provide suggestions, time, and materials for various self-calming strategies, such as those presented below. As with other skills, the goal is for children to eventually do these activities independently, without adult guidance and prompting.

> The greatest weapon against stress is our ability to choose one thought over another.
>
> —William James

- **Breathe deeply.** When anxious or under stress, our natural tendency is to take rapid, shallow breaths. However, science confirms that breathing deeply—by inhaling through the nose, holding the breath for a few seconds, and then exhaling through the mouth—relaxes the cluster of neurons in the brain stem known as the *respiratory pacemaker*. This in turn slows the heart rate and leads to a relaxation response. According to Patricia Gerbarg, author of a 2009 research study, "By changing patterns of breathing, we can change our emotional states and how we think and how we interact with the world" (Kozub 2017). You can help children focus on breathing deeply using these techniques:
  - Count out loud with children each time they take a deep breath, up to four or five.
  - Have children pretend the fingers on their hand are birthday candles. Then have the children blow out each of the five candles.
  - Pretend to blow air into a balloon.
- **Offer a relaxing place to de-stress.** Add soft furnishings to create a calm ambience and lavender, rose, or ylang-ylang essential oils and aromas to appeal to children's sense of smell. Dim the classroom lights and play quiet music. Make this place a haven that sends children the message, "This is a place where you can get away and make yourself feel calm."

- **Visualize calmness.** Have children lie down with one hand on their stomach and the other on their chest. Say, "Close your eyes, and think of your muscles relaxing, from the top of your head to the bottom of your feet. Can you feel your body relaxing? Do you feel calm?"

- **Squeeze out the tension.** Sometimes all it takes to release tension is to tightly hug a stuffed animal or squeeze a ball. Manipulating playdough or clay can have a similar effect. These activities divert the child's focus away from what is bothersome to the physical act of squeezing.

- **Relax with sand and water play.** Just as adults find comfort soaking in a bath or walking on a beach, so too do young children relax when playing with these natural substances. Blowing bubbles, a form of water play, has been found to have particularly calming effects.

- **Commune with nature.** By sitting near trees and closing one's eyes, breathing slows down and relaxation sets in. The Japanese call it *shinrin-yoku*, which means "forest bathing." Researchers at the University of East Anglia analyzed the findings of more than 140 studies involving people from twenty countries. They found that forest bathing not only reduces stress and calms one down, but it also lowers blood pressure, improves one's mood, boosts the immune system, focuses one's attention, increases energy, and improves sleep (Livni 2016; Park et al. 2010).

- **Exercise away the tension.** Outdoor time spent running, climbing, jumping, and throwing allows children to release tension and enjoy moving their bodies and being with others.

- **Dance the stress away.** Like exercise, dancing to lively music helps children de-stress and forget about what is bothering them.

- **Do yoga, stretch, be mindful, and meditate.** All of these activities teach children to self-calm by concentrating on breathing and looking inward, away from the source of anxiety. Research into these practices has shown that they reduce stress, improve focus, give children confidence, boost concentration, instill happiness, and contribute to school success.

Creating an Environment and Structure Where Optimism Can Flourish

In this chapter, we have explored nine optimism-supporting skills. The best way for educators to ensure they are addressing each of these skills is to have a well-planned and responsive environment and program structure. In the chart below, we describe the major elements of a high-quality early childhood setting that sets the stage for the development of these optimism-supporting skills.

Environmental Feature	How This Feature Supports Optimism
Indoor and outdoor areas are free of health and physical dangers; children can safely explore and experiment using all their senses.	*Enables risk taking:* Margot does somersaults on the grass outdoors. When she falls, the soft grass cushions her, and she gets right back up again. (This also supports perseverance and self-efficacy.) *Encourages problem solving:* Tomas and Andrea build a grocery store on a flat carpeted area perfect for block building. (This activity also supports perseverance.)
Materials are displayed on low, open shelving labeled with pictures and words in all languages spoken by children.	*Develops independence:* Carolyn removes the sieve and baster from the shelf by the water table to use in her play. *Promotes executive function:* Emilio and Sissy take a board game from the shelf and put it on the floor. They go over the rules of the game and then decide who will go first. *Develops confidence and self-efficacy:* Bruce gets paper and markers from the shelf, brings them to the table, and uses an alphabet strip as a reference for writing his name and copying letters. (This also supports independence.)
Toys and materials represent the languages and home cultures of all children in the program.	*Promotes empathy:* When Carlos shakes the maracas in time to the music, Dana gets another pair from the shelf, telling Carlos, "That's way cool. I want to play with them too." *Encourages confidence and self-efficacy:* Layla is pleased to find a recipe card to make tuna salad like she makes with her nana at home.
An area in the entryway is designated for exchanging information and communicating with families.	*Promotes empathy:* Salma feels happy to see her father smile when the teacher greets him. *Builds independence:* Franny says, "I'll hang up my coat," while the teacher talks to her mother. *Develops confidence and self-efficacy:* Kenny feels proud when his teacher tells his dad how his son sorted all the Legos by color.

(continued on next page)

Environmental Feature	How This Feature Supports Optimism
The daily schedule includes an hour (or more) of uninterrupted indoor work time when children can choose where to play and work, with whom, and what they will do.	*Supports executive function:* Marcy opts to join others in dramatic play, taking on the role of a mother going to work. (This also builds independence.) *Develops confidence and self-efficacy:* DeMarco chooses a puzzle with more pieces than the one he did yesterday. (This also supports perseverance and problem-solving skills.) *Promotes emotional regulation:* Matthew misses his dad, who works on the night shift. He makes roads in the sand table and works through his sad feelings. (This also supports self-calming.)
An hour or more of outdoor time is scheduled daily, when children are free to pick activities of their choice.	*Facilitates risk taking:* John has been afraid to climb on the monkey bars. But when his friend Pedro beckons him to join him, John slowly attempts climbing up to where Pedro is perched. (This also promotes perseverance.) *Supports emotional regulation:* Eloise feels restless. She starts throwing the horseshoes toward the poles. She exhales deeply and seems to feel much better. (This also supports self-calming skills and self-efficacy.) *Promotes self-calming:* Timothy sits against a tree trunk, looking up at the clouds through the branches and relishing the feeling of the sun and breeze on his cheeks. (This also supports emotional regulation.)
The daily plan includes opportunities for children to play and work by themselves, with a friend, with a small group, or with the whole group.	*Promotes empathy:* When Annie sees Margarite standing alone and looking sad, she asks her if she'd like to paint with her. Margarite nods and smiles broadly. *Encourages problem solving:* Brooklyn and Dawne sit at the computer using a math program. Dawne controls the mouse but isn't sure what to click on to work their way through the program. Brooklyn offers advice, and Dawne tries it. Dawne yells out "Yes!" as the move opens a door on the computer screen.
Group meetings occur in the morning to plan and at the end of the day to review the day's experiences.	*Promotes executive function:* During the morning meeting, the teacher plays some music. She asks the children to move to the rhythm of the beat and synchronize their actions to the words of a song. This improves their working memory and inhibitory skills. *Facilitates problem solving:* Mr. James says, "The bean plants on the windowsill are not growing well. Children, what do you think we should do to help the plants grow?" *Encourages empathy:* During the afternoon meeting, the teacher asks each child to mention one thing they did that day to make a friend feel good.

Environmental Feature	How This Feature Supports Optimism
Space and materials are sufficient, so children can play, work, and carry out plans undisturbed.	*Promotes perseverance:* The paint clumps up on Jackson's first attempt to make leaf prints. He recycles his paper and starts over, this time being more careful with the paint. Happy with his second effort, he asks the teacher to help him hang it on the drying rack. (This also supports risk taking and promotes confidence.) *Encourages problem solving:* Emily spreads out a collection of shells on a tray. She uses a magnifying glass to examine them. She then sorts the shells into piles by color, size, and shape. *Encourages independence:* David is publishing a book about the class field trip to the art museum. He gets a hole punch and yarn from the shelf to bind the pages together. (This also supports confidence and self-efficacy.)
A range of toys, materials, and children's books are available so children of varied abilities and needs can master curricular goals. (See appendix A for a list of age-appropriate optimism-related books to stock your program with.)	*Builds confidence and self-efficacy:* With the teacher, Demarise plays a matching game that is more complex than she is used to. She smiles triumphantly after identifying and naming all the animals found on a farm. *Develops perseverance:* Cameron can catch and throw a beach ball. Now he tries a smaller ball. At first he drops it. But with practice, he learns to throw and catch it. (This also supports risk taking.) *Promotes self-calming:* After Michael fought with Dallas, the teacher suggests that Michael visit the calming corner. When the teacher joins him, she finds that Michael is quite agitated and not willing to talk. The teacher sits next to Michael and begins reading *Charlotte and the Quiet Place* by Deborah Sosin to him. As she reads, the teacher encourages Michael to take calming breaths, as Charlotte does.

The nine skills featured in this chapter set the tone for optimistic thinking. To teach optimism, it's important to make sure the program recognizes the importance of these skills and nourishes them through the program's philosophy, physical space, and daily schedule.

The next step is to make use of this optimism-supporting climate to actually teach children the skill of thinking optimistically.

CHAPTER 4

Activities for Building Children's Optimism

[In the early childhood years] we constantly introduce new vocabulary,
model expected behaviors, and expose children to new ideas. It's the perfect
time to introduce the mechanics of optimistic thinking.

—Terri Granger, Pre-K Teacher

Everything you've read thus far in this book has been preparation for this chapter. Here we cover what you can do in your work with children to enhance optimistic thinking. These activities are the very heart of teaching children to think optimistically. The practices you introduce, teach, and reinforce can make the difference in children's lives.

Helping children develop optimistic explanatory styles is a gradual process. You can help children begin this process by encouraging them to dispute negative thinking and substitute pessimistic thoughts with flexible, optimistic ones. To do this, you'll need to use the ABCDE model introduced in chapter 2. This should be regarded as an ongoing activity that educators use day in and day out. It is the first and most important thing you can do to lead children to optimistic thinking. Whenever you hear a child expressing pessimism ("I can't do it" or "No one wants to play with me" or "I miss out on all the fun"), it is time to have a conversation and go through the five steps of the ABCDE process.

This chapter describes twelve activities for teaching preschool and kindergarten children to think optimistically. Individually and cumulatively, these activities will support and reinforce your everyday use of the ABCDE model.

The activities are meant to be integrated into your ongoing curriculum, not taught as a one-time, separate unit on optimism. Since optimism is a thinking style and an approach to life, it is something to weave into your program, returning to it again and again.

The activities do not need to be used in a specific order. You can pick and choose which ones to use and when to use them. Some of the activities are appropriate for individual children, others lend themselves to small-group activities, and still others are appropriate for the whole class. It's up to you to adapt the activities to fit the characteristics of individuals and the group and your own teaching style.

Each activity description includes steps for implementation, an example of the activity in action, follow-up ideas, and suggestions for engaging families. Family engagement is an important part of all early childhood programs. When educators and family members forge meaningful partnerships, children have better outcomes. By exchanging information about the child's activities, experiences, interests, and interactions both at the program and at home, teachers and family members can ensure that the child is optimally growing, developing, and learning. Additional information on engaging families appears in appendix B along with family-friendly versions of six of these activities.

The inspiration for these activities comes primarily from Dr. Martin Seligman, particularly through his two pivotal books *Learned Optimism* (2006) and *The Optimistic Child* (2007). Several activities are based on ideas from Canada's Reaching IN…Reaching OUT Program (RIRO), which was developed in concert with University of Pennsylvania staff, including Dr. Karen Reivich. Many of the activity ideas are original to the authors of this book.

You will note that there is some overlap between the optimism activities presented here and the related concepts presented in chapter 1—resilience, mindfulness, growth mindset, grit, happiness, kindness, and gratitude. This is because optimism is integral to all these concepts. Thus, for instance, teaching gratitude automatically promotes the development of optimism.

In addition, these activities overlap with the skills children develop in an optimistic program climate, as discussed in chapter 3. Emotional regulation, executive function, self-efficacy, independence, risk taking, perseverance, problem solving, empathy, and self-calming are all foundational to optimistic thinking. Thus much of what you learned in that chapter will carry over to these activities.

To ensure that these activities are effective and work as intended, they were field-tested in a diverse group of early childhood programs. The teachers and children in the pilot test represented public, military, and private programs, including Head Start and the Department of Defense Education Activity overseas program Sure Start (which is based on the Head Start model). The early childhood education settings include those that are federally funded, state sponsored, faith based, and privately owned. The programs serve various socioeconomic populations in urban, suburban, and rural locales in California, in the Midwest, and on the East Coast, and in Department of Defense schools in Italy, Korea, and Japan. Comments from the teachers who tested the activities and generously shared their feedback with the authors appear throughout this chapter and chapter 2. (A list of these teachers appears in the acknowledgments section of this book.)

By incorporating these twelve activities into your ongoing program, you can help children develop healthy, optimistic thinking that will benefit them in school and life. Here is how one teacher who participated in the field test summarized her experience and its impact on the children she teaches (Eileen Ricardo, pers. comm.): "The optimism-building activities we field-tested helped students problem solve, persevere, and think more optimistically and make positive choices. Although we always knew that these were important skills for children to learn, finding a way 'how' to teach these skills had always been a challenge up until now."

Create Optimistic Endings to Stories That Present a Problem or Challenge

In this activity, young children can use their imaginations and their knowledge of optimism to lead a character in a story to an optimistic ending that addresses a challenge.

Steps

1. Make up and record a story about a child who is struggling with a problem. You might begin with the sample story below.
2. Listen to or read the story aloud together with the children. Pause to ask and answer questions or underscore key points.
3. Build on the story by asking children to take on the perspective of the main character. Ask questions such as those in the example: "How can Jorge figure out a plan that will work well in the future?" Lead children in reviewing how to make optimistic choices.
4. Ask follow-up questions, listen to responses, and guide the conversation toward an optimistic conclusion to the story. For the sample story, an optimistic outcome might build on Jorge's strengths. Jorge may still be in the beginning stages of block building, but what is something else that he does well? Engage children in developing a plan for Jorge that will lead to his making positive choices rather than becoming frustrated and angry.

Example

The Story of Jorge the Builder

Jorge, age four, loves to build with blocks. Jamal and Marta, also four, are block-building experts. Every day they build complicated constructions.

One day Jamal builds a space station and Marta builds a highway with cars. Ms. Martin, their teacher, takes photos and posts them on the classroom wall. Their classmates say, "Ooh" and "Wow."

Jorge thinks, "I wish I could build stuff like Jamal and Marta." But he can't. Instead he builds small towers and bridges. And they fall down more often than not.

The next day, Marta, Jamal, and Jorge are playing in the block area. Jorge looks at the huge buildings Marta and Jamal are making. Then he looks at his bridge and thinks, "My bridge is just small and stupid." He gets very upset.

"I can't build anything!" he yells, knocking the blocks. They fly across the block area. Luckily no one is hurt.

Ms. Martin sits next to Jorge. In a calm voice, she asks, "What's going on, Jorge? You know someone could be hurt from flying blocks. What were you thinking about in your head when you threw the blocks?"

Now it's your turn: What do you think Jorge said to Ms. Martin? How do you think Jorge felt about what happened? How can Jorge figure out a plan that will work well in the future?

Follow-up

1. Write additional stories, ideally based on challenges observed among the children you teach. For example, there might be a child who doesn't want to join group meetings, a child who becomes frustrated trying to learn to write his name, or a child who is sad because her best friend moved away.
2. Follow the process outlined above to reach an optimistic conclusion.

Engaging Families

1. Ask families to share anonymous examples of challenges children faced at home that could be handled with optimistic thinking. Turn these sample challenges into stories to share in the classroom.
2. Give families copies of handout 5 from appendix B so they can do a family version of this activity at home. Post it online too if you have a classroom web page or blog.

We used our Piggie and Gerald [characters in the Elephant & Piggie series by Mo Willems] puppets to tell the Jorge story. The children focused on the rule the character had broken and could say how he felt. The problem solving was a little harder, but several four-year-olds offered good answers. Avynn said, "They need to do teamwork." Alec said, "He needs to have the other guy hold it while he builds." Bentlee said, "Just keep trying."

—Sarah Bollingmo, Preschool Site Supervisor

ACTIVITY 2

Put on Skits or Puppet Shows That Highlight Optimistic Thinking

Taking on the role of a character lets children step out of themselves and see situations through a different lens. Children in the audience learn from seeing optimistic thinking in action. (Note: This activity is based on an idea from Pearson and Hall 2017.)

Steps

1. Select three puppets or dolls to represent the following characters: a child the same age as the children in the classroom, a teacher, and a narrator.
2. Choose a participant to assume the role of the child character. He can give the puppet/doll a name, including his own. (In the example below, the child puppet is named David.) Review the basic premise for the show: What is David upset about?
3. Assume the role of both the teacher and narrator, using the appropriate puppets/dolls. Although you typically do not play a leading role in puppet shows or skits, you need to serve as a model for this activity. You can act out how a teacher might help a child facing this challenge.
4. Invite a small group of three or four children to be the audience. If the participating child is comfortable performing in front of a larger audience, then invite more children.
5. Following the presentation, ask the children the questions below. Help the children understand the reasons why David's problem is temporary and limited in scope, and encourage them to focus on its optimistic outcome.
   a. What was the problem?
   b. How do you think David felt?
   c. How did the teacher help David talk through what was bothering him?
   d. How did the teacher guide David to change his thinking about the problem?
   e. Why are things not always as bad as they seem?
6. Invite the children in the audience to put on their own version of this puppet show/skit using the narrator, teacher, and child puppets/dolls. Then debrief with the children about how they helped the child think about the situation in a more optimistic way.

Example

David Feels Left Out

Narrator: Once there was a school where children came to play and learn. David is a child in the preschool class. David, take a bow and introduce yourself.

David: *(Bows.)* I am four. I have a baby sister. *(Then hangs head and looks sad.)*

Narrator: What's going on? David is frowning. He looks sad. He is sitting by himself, watching his friends happily playing. David feels left out.

Teacher: David, you look sad. Are you unhappy? What are you thinking to yourself?

David: I want to play, but there's no room for me.

Teacher: It sounds like you are sad because nobody is playing with you. Is that what's making you unhappy?

David: *(Nods.)* Yes.

Teacher: I understand why that makes you feel bad. It hurts when no one wants to play with us. But this doesn't happen all the time. Just this morning I saw you and Angie examining pinecones together. You were both laughing. You looked like two friends having fun. Were you?

David: *(Nods.)* I had fun with Angie. She is my friend.

Teacher: I think you might feel disappointed because you're not playing with Angie right now. That doesn't mean you'll always play alone, though. Sometimes you do play by yourself, but many times you play with Angie or another friend. And sometimes our whole class plays together. Remember when we had a marching band? Also, sometimes you play with me. Would you like to sit with me now and make plans for the rest of the day?

David: *(Nods.)* Yes. I want to play marching band outdoors.

Narrator: Looks like things are turning around for David. Things aren't always as bad as they seem. Everyone can take a bow now. *(David, Teacher, and Narrator bow.)*

Follow-up

1. Encourage children to present other puppet shows or skits that deal with their thoughts about adverse situations. Try to use scenarios that have occurred or might occur in your class. For example:
   a. a child can't keep up with other children doing physical activities;
   b. a newcomer to the class feels that she doesn't fit in;
   c. several children are sad when the volcano-eruption experiment doesn't work.
2. Have the children select and use the puppets/dolls to act out the situation. The teacher puppet/doll can help the child puppet/doll keep or change those feelings, as appropriate.
3. Video record these presentations so children can revisit them on their own. The more frequently children see themselves (and puppets and dolls) conquering problems and talking to themselves optimistically, the more likely they will be to adopt these behaviors in their own lives.

Engaging Families

1. Share the videos of the children's presentations with families if appropriate.
2. Offer families instructions for making different kinds of puppets and dolls using simple materials found at home—paper bags, socks, towels, yarn, paper towel rolls, and so on. Encourage families to use the puppets/dolls to encourage optimistic thinking.
3. Give families copies of handout 6 from appendix B so they can do a family version of this activity at home. Post it online too if you have a classroom web page or blog.

This was awesome. The children really got into the play. Some of the subjects that grabbed their attention were

- a nonreader comparing herself to a reader
- a child who can't draw seeing the amazing drawing done by a child nearby
- a child who can't climb the monkey bars, thinking he will never be able to do it

—Joanna Phinney, Kindergarten Teacher

ACTIVITY 3

Use Persona Dolls to Reinforce Optimistic Thinking

Persona dolls differ from dolls in the dramatic play center in that they are considered members of the classroom or program. They can range in size from typical doll size (about twelve inches) to toddler size (wearing size 2T clothing). Persona dolls hang out wherever children engage in activities, and the dolls become part of daily life.

With a teacher's help, the dolls can tell stories about their own lives and share their feelings. Typically educators use persona dolls to teach children about diversity, but they can also be used to teach skills, such as learning to think optimistically.

Steps

1. Purchase, make, or transform dolls already in your program into persona dolls. (Consult the resources listed on page 64.) Consider gender, race, culture, body type, disabilities, and other unique physical characteristics. Start with one or two persona dolls, and add more dolls over time. The goal is to represent diversity as found in your setting.

2. Introduce one doll at a time during group time. You can involve the children in naming and creating a background story for the doll, or you can do this yourself to focus on a specific goal. The following are possible details to consider: Who are the doll's family members? Where does she live? How long has the family lived in this community or country? Try to represent the backgrounds of the children in the class and community.

3. Tell the children a short story about the doll's life before she came to their classroom. Invite the children to ask questions. Explain that the doll can join in their play experiences.

4. Ask the children where they would like the doll to "live" in the classroom. This should be somewhere accessible to everyone.

5. Observe children to see how they include the persona doll in their daily activities. Some children may need guidance on how the persona doll is different from the ones they're used to playing with.

Persona Dolls Resources

For more information about persona dolls:

- http://eyfs.info/articles.html/general/persona-dolls-r127
- www.teachingforchange.org/wp-content/uploads/2012/08/ec_personadolls_english.pdf

To create persona dolls:

- https://prezi.com/gkqjse-hpexg/how-to-create-a-persona-doll/?webgl=0
- http://personadoll.uk/creating-personas

Here's how one classroom worked with a textile designer to turn the children's sketches into persona dolls. The teacher divided the class into two groups. Each group was charged with coming up with a design for a persona doll that could become part of their classroom. The groups chose each doll's gender, age, skin color, eye color, hairstyle and color, and clothing. They then made a crayon drawing of what they wanted the persona doll to look like. The designer transformed the children's drawings into sketches and actual dolls. The finished dolls were Elizabeth, age five, and Jaymark, age four. Elizabeth and Jaymark became beloved community members.

 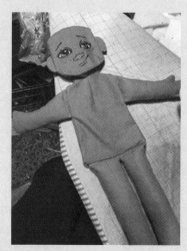 

To turn regular dolls into persona dolls:

The Little Book of Persona Dolls by Marilyn Bowles (2004)

To purchase persona dolls:

- Consult school supply companies
- www.etsy.com/market/persona_doll

6. Encourage children to interact with the persona doll as they might another classmate. When a problem or challenge arises, invite the child to discuss the situation with you and the persona doll, as Marcus does in the example below. Taking on the voice of the persona doll, gently lead the child to challenge pessimistic thinking and take on a more optimistic viewpoint.

Example

Henry the Doll Helps Out When Marcus Misses Outdoor Time

TEACHER: Good morning, Marcus. How was your doctor's appointment?

MARCUS: Fine, but I'm mad. I missed outdoor playtime. I always miss the fun things.

TEACHER: Sometimes Henry feels that way too. *(Henry sits in the teacher's lap.)*

HENRY: I know what you mean. Sometimes I think I never have fun. But then I remember in my head that I *have* had fun times.

TEACHER: I know it can seem that way, boys. But I've seen Marcus having fun before.

HENRY: Me too. I saw him have fun yesterday. He and Jessie were doing somersaults.

MARCUS: Henry has a great memory. He's right. It was fun doing somersaults. I'll look for Jessie so we can do some more after naptime.

TEACHER AND HENRY: Way to go, Marcus! You have a good memory too.

MARCUS: I know. I need to remember to use it! Henry, can you sit with me at lunchtime?

HENRY: Sure!

Follow-up

1. Continue using the doll to tell learned optimism stories at group time. Keep the stories relatively simple at first, then add content related to the doll's learning to face problems by thinking optimistically. Try to incorporate

difficult experiences similar to those the children in the group have experienced and handled. Discuss what happens in the stories and help children identify the optimistic strategies the persona doll uses to overcome challenges.

2. Add new dolls with different characteristics and personalities over time. Match the dolls' characteristics and experiences to those of the children in the group, particularly children who are still learning to use optimistic thinking. Introduce the new dolls to the children at group time (again, one at a time). Repeat the process described above.

Engaging Families

1. Encourage children to introduce the persona dolls to their families at pickup and drop-off times and through photos and short smartphone or tablet videos.

2. Ask for volunteers with sewing and design skills to help make new dolls.

Using the persona dolls, we discussed how to help each other when we have problems. We are still smart even if we have a problem, and we can solve any problem because we are creative problem solvers!

—Therese Fitzgerald, Sure Start Teacher

I had never heard of persona dolls before, and this activity became our own mini-project in my classroom. From designing to introducing the dolls, every step has gone well! The children enjoyed thinking about the dolls' culture, individual features, ages, and names.

We are still developing the life stories of the dolls, and the children are beginning to include them in their play, during conflict resolution, and throughout our daily routine. The dolls have really become members of our community.

—Peggy DeLanghe, Master Pre-K Teacher

ACTIVITY 4

Encourage Dramatic Play Scenarios That Rely on Optimistic Thinking

Young children come up with many meaningful play scenarios on their own. But in this activity, teachers step in to suggest scenarios that include challenges to be addressed through optimistic thinking.

Steps

1. Visit the dramatic play center and suggest a few scenarios the children might want to act out. Here are some sample scenarios:
   a. The children are playing "restaurant," and one customer doesn't like his veggie burger.
   b. "Mom" must go away for work, and everyone in the family is upset.
   c. A "family" learns that rain is predicted for Saturday, when they have plans to picnic with their relatives.
2. Join in the play to ensure that children are learning to resolve the situation positively. Typically teachers leave children to engage in dramatic play on their own, but here you can step in to model language and behaviors. If things aren't going in an optimistic direction, ask questions and make statements to help turn things around.
3. Discuss with the children how they feel about the play scenario and how it was resolved. Ask, "How does it feel to have successfully resolved the problem?" and "Does thinking optimistically make you feel good about yourself?"
4. Invite children to act out other optimism-related dramatic play scenarios.

Example

What If It Rains?

A teacher encourages several children to act out the rainy-day scenario suggested above. The children take on the roles of family members faced with the challenge of their Saturday picnic being rained out. During play, their teacher poses questions and offers comments such as the following:

- "What were you thinking in your head that made you upset?"
- "I know you're disappointed, but we can make a new plan for our get-together."
- "How did you figure out what else the family can do?"
- "We can still have the same foods we were going to eat outdoors inside."
- "What foods and activities can we enjoy inside that we couldn't have enjoyed if the picnic had been outdoors?"
- "What else could we do to prepare for an indoor picnic?"
- "There are lots of family members working together to plan a fun day."
- "It's great that we have a dry place to go where we can eat and play games and have fun together."

Follow-up

1. Invite a different group of children to perform the same scenario, with the first group watching as an audience.
2. Lead the performers and the audience in comparing the direction their stories took. What was similar and what was different about the two performances? Stress the idea that the outcomes of the stories don't have to be identical. In real life, there's usually more than one successful answer to a problem. The important thing is to resolve the problem optimistically.

Engaging Families

1. Share with families the sample questions that appear above. Suggest they have family discussions about situations when an optimistic outlook could turn an adverse event into a happy one. They can consider this to be practice for actual adverse situations.
2. Encourage families to involve their children in planning how to get past an actual adverse situation and turn it around with optimistic thinking.

Scenarios we acted out included the following:

- There is a new baby in the home. The baby can't play with us, cries a lot, sleeps a lot, eats a lot, and takes up a lot of Mom's and Dad's time.
- The air quality and freezing cold temperatures have made it impossible to be able to play outside.
- A child forgot to bring his blanket to school for rest time.
- A child doesn't get to play in a chosen interest area. This happened two days in a row due to others choosing the area first.

We focused on what we can do versus what we can't do. The kids use their "happy [optimism] goggles" (fingers around their eyes like glasses) to help them remember this.

—Tonya Grant, Early Childhood Educator

Read Aloud and Discuss Books That Focus on Optimism

In this activity, teachers read aloud books that either lend themselves to discussions about optimistic thinking or have a specific focus on optimism or a related skill. The read-aloud sessions are followed by meaningful conversations about the characters' choices and about the benefits of optimistic thinking.

Steps

1. Choose a book related to optimism. While you probably have your own favorites, you'll find a list of suggestions in appendix A. Read the book aloud, all the way through, at least once at group time and one-on-one with individual children.

2. Read the book together again with the same group or individuals as before. This time stop frequently to ask pertinent questions and engage children in the process of analyzing a problem. Discuss the choices the main characters make, whether their reactions are based on facts or fears, and how to resolve the problem optimistically. You can tailor your questions to fit the story and the children.

    a. What happened to _____ in this story?

    b. How did this make _____ feel?

    c. What do you suppose _____ was thinking inside his/her head?

    d. What would you say to _____?

    e. What would you have suggested that _____ do?

    f. How did _____ think things through?

    g. What plan did _____ come up with?

    h. What do you think will happen next time _____ has a problem?

    i. Would you have ended the story like this? If not, how would you end the book? Why did you pick this ending?

3. Relate the main characters' experiences to those of the children. Make sure the children understand the book's message and how thinking optimistically makes life better.

4. Repeat the steps with the children (both one-on-one and with groups) reading aloud as many books as you can fit into your daily program.

Example

When Pigs Fly

Mr. Tozzi chooses the book *When Pigs Fly* by Valerie Coulman to read aloud with the children. During and after the second reading, he asks questions such as the following:

1. How do you think Ralph felt when his dad said, "No, no, no," to his request for a bike? Why wasn't Ralph angry or sad?
2. What was Ralph thinking in his head when his dad said, "When pigs fly"?
3. What would you have done if you were Ralph? What plan did Ralph come up with?
4. Why do you think Ralph thought he could do things that people told him were impossible?
5. How do you think Ralph felt when the pigs flew in the helicopter?
6. How was Ralph able to change his dad's mind?
7. How did it help Ralph to think in his head that he could do whatever he set his mind to?
8. Would you always like to think happy thoughts like Ralph? Why or why not? Is thinking happy thoughts hard to do?
9. How does the story make you feel?
10. What could Ralph do in the future?

Follow-up

1. Encourage children to retell and act out the stories you read aloud with them. Provide props and puppets so they can make the experience come alive.
2. Suggest alternative scenarios to act out that might test the main character's optimism.

Engaging Families

1. Create a lending library of book bags with optimism-related books. Encourage families to first read the story all the way through and then reread it with time for questions. Include suggested discussion questions for second and subsequent readings. Also include a journal so children and families

can share their responses to the questions with others who also borrow the book bags.

2. Share appendix A with families. Point out which of the books on the list are particular favorites of the program and of their child.

3. Give families copies of handout 7 in appendix B so they can do a family version of this activity at home. Post it online too if you have a classroom web page or blog.

We read aloud the book *Pete the Cat and His Magic Sunglasses* by Kimberly and James Dean. The class loves Pete the Cat books, and we hadn't read that one yet. They enjoy the repetition and the song-like elements. This one had a great chant for them to repeat on positivity and optimism. We made magic sunglasses with our hands, which the children put on while reading. And then we discussed if we needed sunglasses to reframe our perspective.

I also asked the children to help me as I pretended to be grouchy, sad, mad, and frustrated. Many of them offered me sunglasses and then asked if I would play with them.

—Cassandra Redding, Head Start Teacher

After reading *Pete the Cat and His Magic Sunglasses* to a large group, we discussed the book as well as scenarios that may have left the children feeling bad. When guided to talk about situations where they felt bad in some way, they had solutions to solving problems and moving on with a better feeling.

—Dawn Smith, Master Preschool Teacher

ACTIVITY 6

Use Illustrations to Create Stories about Optimistic Thinking

Sometimes a picture truly is worth a thousand words, as shown in this activity. Here children examine the details of an illustration and focus on the challenges the depicted individual(s) might be facing. They then use their observations to create and tell a story. (Note: This activity is based on an idea from Pearson and Hall 2017.)

Steps

1. Select a book on optimism you haven't yet read aloud to the children. (See appendix A.)
2. Choose an illustration from the book—preferably one of an individual person or several people or animals displaying emotion or overt action—and then show it to the children.
3. Lead children in making up a story based on this one illustration. Encourage them to focus on the feelings of the person(s) or animal(s) in their story and what challenges they may be facing. Review the character(s)' decisions and discuss how these choices are examples of optimistic thinking. (Note: Some younger children may tell stories from books they are familiar with, rather than making up an original story. This is fine. Use whatever story they are telling to point out optimistic thinking.)
4. Record the storytelling performances so children can revisit them.
5. Have the participants give themselves a hand for a story well told.

Example

Ms. Chowdhurry and the Children Make Up a Story

Ms. Chowdhurry selects an illustration from a new book. She says, "Let's make up a story about the people and things in this picture." She starts out the story, "Once upon a time there was..." Next, she asks questions to help the children come up with a story:

1. What's happening in this picture? Who do you see? What is everyone doing?
2. How are the people/animals in the picture feeling? What's making them feel this way?
3. What are they saying to themselves about what is happening? What do you imagine they are thinking in their heads?
4. How might this make others feel?
5. What will happen next? What else might the characters in the story do?
6. How will their choices make the people/animals feel?

As the children create their story, Ms. Chowdhurry helps them think of choices for the characters that could lead to optimistic thinking. By encouraging them to think of "happy things" that might happen next, the children develop a positive outcome for the characters in their story.

Follow-up

1. Repeat the activity with a variation:
   a. Show children a photograph and ask them to come up with a story about what the people in the photo are thinking and feeling. Begin with a photo of the child (or children) with whom you are doing this activity. The photo should show the child/children engaged in an activity or interacting with classmates.
   b. Encourage the child/children to make up a story rather than try to remember what was actually happening when the photo was taken. However, if the child/children can't make the transition from what did happen in the photo, accept whatever story they relate.
   c. Follow up using photos of strangers engaged in activities and expressing emotions as the basis for storytelling.
2. Ask children questions such as those noted above, and lead them to incorporate choices and decisions into their story that lead to optimistic thinking. Again, record the story so that the storyteller can revisit it.

Engaging Families

1. Tell families about this activity and how the children responded. Suggest they use some family photos or other photos or illustrations to repeat the activity at home. They are likely to learn a lot about their child's ability to recall events, make up stories, and use optimistic thinking.

2. Post some interesting photos of people on the classroom website and invite families to discuss them with their children using the questions listed above.

I showed a child a picture of smiling children lined up on a baseball field. He made up a story about how all the children were happy except for one, who was hungry and thirsty. According to the storyteller, the unhappy child went to a water fountain to drink some water and then got some food to eat. The unhappy child was now happy again!

—Virginia Weaver, Teacher and Site Supervisor

ACTIVITY 7

Help Children Write and Illustrate Books about Optimistic Thinking

In this activity, children apply their writing and drawing skills to reinforce and build on their understanding of optimism. The result is a book to share with classmates and family members.

Steps

1. Plan an approach to bookmaking to use with the children. Questions such as the following can help you plan:
   a. Will children use the computer or paper and writing tools? Will you be the transcriber who writes or types the story?
   b. Will children use the story from activity 6, create a new one, or write their own version of a book you have read aloud and discussed? If you choose the latter option, pick a book you read to children in activity 5, and encourage children to either rewrite the story or come up with another alternative ending that is also optimistic.
   c. Will children work alone, with a partner, or as part of a small group of authors?
   d. How will children illustrate the story? Will they use art materials to draw or paint? Will they use collage, by cutting out and pasting pictures or photos? Or will they use a drawing program on the computer? (If you have a story-writing program, children can produce the entire book on the computer.)
2. Explain the activity to the children and provide the materials, time, and support needed to create their books. The length and number of illustrations should be determined by the authors.
3. Help the children, as needed, turn their stories into finished books. To bind the book, children can either staple pages or punch holes and string yarn or shoelaces through the holes to keep the pages together.
4. Demonstrate how to make a special cover using cardboard or thick stock paper that can be laminated. Make sure the author's and illustrator's name or names are prominently displayed on the cover.

5. Have children share their finished books with the class, then place them in the classroom library. To the right are some sample pages from books created by preschoolers.

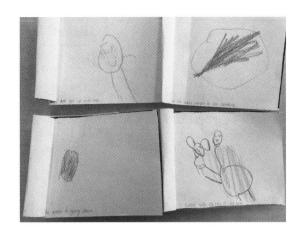

Example

To illustrate, a story that could be turned into a book is shown here. This rewritten story is based on the book *The Hyena Who Lost Her Laugh* by Jessica Lamb-Shapiro. Of course, children's versions will be simpler and in their own words.

The Hyena Who Lost Her Laugh

A New Version

Hillary the Hyena loved to laugh. It was a great laugh too. She laughed all the time.

Once she had a bad day at school. Her best friend, Abigail, didn't want to play. Her tomato plants died. Jamie said Hillary's singing was too loud. The puzzle was too hard, and she couldn't finish it. Lunch wasn't very tasty, either.

When she got home, she went straight to her room.

Mommy Hyena knocked on Hillary's door and asked, "Is everything okay in there? I don't hear any laughing, Hillary."

"I'm not in a laughing mood," said Hillary. "I can't do anything right. No one likes me. School's too hard."

"I hope you do laugh again," said Mom. "You do a lot of things right. You can throw and catch a ball. You paint amazing pictures. But most of all, you have the best laugh of any hyena I've ever known."

"How many hyenas do you know, Mom?" asked Hillary.

"Well, there's you and me," said Mom, smiling.

Hillary started to laugh. Her laugh started out small but got bigger and bigger as she kept laughing.

Hillary's mom grinned proudly and said, "That's my hyena girl."

"I guess I can do a lot more things than I thought!" said Hillary.

Follow-up

1. Create audiobook versions of the stories.
2. Use the children's books for read-alouds from time to time.
3. Help children find props and costumes so they can act out the books.
4. Make a video recording of the children's performances to share on the class website.

Engaging Families

1. Encourage children to share the books they made with their families. They can take them home and read them together.
2. Provide materials and instructions for making more books at home. Modify instructions so they are as simple as possible, and encourage families to use items typically found at home.

> The children drew pictures using colored pencils, crayons, and markers. Some wrote their own sentences with inventive spelling, while others dictated their sentences to us.
>
> —Terilyn Stephens, Kindergarten Teacher

ACTIVITY 8

Help Children Learn to Plan before Acting to Encourage Success

This activity can help children learn to think first and make sure they have what they need to succeed. Planning in advance can avoid frustration that leads to pessimistic thinking.

Steps

1. Consider the planning skills of the children in the class and identify those children who need help learning to plan. Some children are constant planners who then run out of time to implement their plans and end up feeling frustrated. Others have vague ideas, dive right in without planning, get upset, and may start thinking pessimistically. The objective is to find a balance between being able to plan and being able to implement that plan.
2. Meet with these children face-to-face and discuss their ideas and goals.
3. Help the children think about what they need to carry out their ideas. This could include materials (Is everything they need already at hand?), time (Will it take an hour or days?), skills (Do they already have the skills needed, or are they still developing them?), and other people (Is this something for one or more than one person?).
4. Provide less and less support as children become skilled planners on their own.

Example

Gwen Plans to Build a House

TEACHER: *(Going up to Gwen in the block center.)* Hi, Gwen. Tell me about your idea.

GWEN: I want to build a house. Then I can play in it with Darnell.

TEACHER: That's an interesting idea. What will you need to build it?

GWEN: We can use all the wooden blocks. There are lots of them.

TEACHER: Hmm . . . If you used all the blocks, I think the other children would be unhappy. There would be no blocks left for them to use.

GWEN: But I want to build a house!

TEACHER: What else could you use to make a house?

GWEN: We could put sheets over a table.

TEACHER: That could work. We have some extra sheets in the closet. What does Darnell think?

GWEN: I'll ask him!

(Gwen and Darnell make their house and have a great time playing in it. At pickup time, the teacher overhears Gwen tell her granddad about the activity.)

GWEN: I'm glad we didn't make our house out of blocks. It would have been unfair to the other children.

Follow-up

1. Create a chart showing the steps in planning: 1. What do you want to do? 2. Where will you do it? 3. What resources do you need? 4. What skills are needed? 5. How many people will it take? 6. How long will it take? Hang the chart in the classroom to remind children what to think about before moving forward with an idea.
2. Comment when children apply their planning skills. Point out how the planning led to successful outcomes while minimizing frustration.

Engaging Families

1. Describe this activity to families and suggest they try it at home. They can model the planning process by talking while getting ready to do something. "First, I need to see if we have enough eggs to make pancakes. Then . . ." Explain that the goal is to show how planning ahead can avoid the kind of frustration that leads to negative thinking.
2. Provide copies of the planning chart for families to post at home.
3. Give families copies of handout 8 from appendix B so they can do a family version of this activity at home. Post it online too if you have a classroom web page or blog.

"

Helping children plan before acting encourages success. It helps the children's understanding because they can physically see the situation they need to work on.

—Allison Wood, Associate Preschool Teacher

"

"

I introduced this activity by reviewing one of our positivity posters: *If Plan A doesn't work, try Plan B. If that doesn't work, try Plan C. Don't give up.*

We then discussed why it is important to plan. I used myself as an example of why I must plan. If I did not plan what to do each day, they might not know what they should be doing. Then we talked about what would happen if someone just started a project without thinking about what they need to do or what they needed. We discussed how someone could become frustrated because maybe they do not know what to do, or they may not have the materials they need. We then made a chart about what planning would look like.

—Eileen Ricardo, Kindergarten Teacher

"

ACTIVITY 9

Make Optimism Part of the Conflict-Resolution Process

Learning to solve problems and resolve conflicts in a positive way are foundational skills for being an optimistic thinker. Help children use this process when disagreements arise. Eventually they will be able to use it on their own.

Steps

1. **Slow down and talk.** Find a quiet place to sit and talk with those involved in the problem situation. This place should be away from the area where the conflict took place. If only two children are involved, sit one on either side of you.

2. **Discuss what happened.** Say to each child, "Tell [use the name of the other child] what just happened." Have the children talk to each other, not you. The child talking gets to tell her perspective about what happened without interruption. Everyone must listen to the speaker, and each child gets a turn to speak.

3. **State the problem.** After everyone has had a turn to speak, summarize what was said and acknowledge and accept each child's feelings. Point out how each child may have hurt the other's feelings without meaning to. Have the children reflect on how their actions affected the other person.

4. **Describe and then agree on what needs to be resolved.** Agree on and implement a plan. Ask the children what they might do to resolve things optimistically. What do they wish would happen? Have each child think of a plan to make things better that includes everyone involved.

5. **Discuss the plans the children came up with.** What are the pros and cons of each child's proposed plan? Ask questions that will steer the children toward a positive, optimistic resolution. Help children work together to agree on a plan that they think will work well. Then put the plan into action.

6. **Evaluate the solution.** After the plan has been implemented, meet with the children to reflect on how well it worked. Were the goals met optimistically? Did the plan work as intended? Ask the children whether they are happy with the results. If not, what should they do now? What plan should they try next? If the plan worked well, congratulate the children on coming up with a solution that benefits everyone.

7. **Observe.** Watch, listen, and learn how well the children's plan is working. If problems persist, repeat steps 5 and 6. Once again, lead children toward an optimistic resolution.

Example

Isabella and Tassneem Test Their Friendship

Isabella is in the dramatic play area wearing a long dress so she can be a "teacher." She calls to her friend Tassneem, who is nearby painting a mural with Billy and Eduardo.

Isabella: Come play school with me.

Tassneem: No. I don't want to play school. I'm busy.

Isabella: I won't be your best friend anymore.

Tassneem: So what?

(An angry Isabella walks to Tassneem and pushes her so hard that she falls and her paint tips over. Tassneem cries. Ms. Barrett, the children's teacher, comes over, picks up the paint container, and comforts Tassneem. Tassneem stops crying.)

Ms. Barrett: Tassneem and Isabella, please come sit with me at the table and talk about what happened. You can each have a turn explaining what happened. Isabella, you can start. Please look at Tassneem while talking to her. Tassneem, please listen to Isabella.

Isabella: You were mean to me. You wouldn't come play with me. I needed you to play school with me, and you wouldn't come.

Ms. Barrett: Thank you, Isabella. Now it's your turn, Tassneem.

Tassneem: I was busy painting with Billy and Eduardo. We were having fun. I didn't want to stop.

Ms. Barrett: I understand why you were upset, Isabella. Your feelings were hurt because you had no one to play school with. Tassneem, can you understand how Isabella might have been sad and angry?

Tassneem: Yeah. But then she said something mean and pushed me.

Ms. Barrett: Isabella, even though you were mad, you know that in our class we don't hurt anyone or anything. If you were angry, you could have told me about it, punched the balls, or thrown beanbags at the target. It's okay to feel mad, but it's not okay to push Tassneem or anyone else.

ISABELLA: I understand. I'm sorry.

MS. BARRETT: I know you feel bad. What could you do to make things better so that you and Tassneem will both be happy? What would you like to happen, Isabella?

ISABELLA: I want to be friends with Tassneem.

MS. BARRETT: And you, Tassneem?

TASSNEEM: I want to be friends with Isabella too.

(Next they discuss and plan what to do to avoid future disagreements—be nice and be patient. The girls clean up the spilled paint together.)

Follow-up

1. Suggest similar scenarios with conflicts in them for children to act out during dramatic play.
2. Encourage children to use persona dolls in helping them reach optimistic conclusions when conflicts arise.
3. Provide opportunities for children to practice real-life conflict resolution on their own, without teacher intervention.

Engaging Families

1. Create a chart that outlines the steps in the conflict resolution process described above. (See Steps.)
2. Post the conflict resolution chart on the families' bulletin board and share paper copies so families can use it at home. Also post it on any online communication venue you use, such as a website, blog, or newsletter. Encourage families to use this process to resolve disagreements at home. Invite them to share the results with you.

"

Over the course of the year, I teach the children to stop and listen and then give affirmation by telling their friends, "I hear what you are saying, and I understand [or am trying to understand] why you are upset." Then we work through the problem. It has been rewarding to hear parents and other adults comment on how their children can work through conflicts with a positive outlook. This demonstrates that the children's skills are carried into their home and life outside of school!

—Tonya Grant, Early Childhood Educator

"

ACTIVITY 10

Encourage Children to Express Optimism through the Visual Arts

This activity is relatively easy to implement because it is likely you already have the materials needed and a time in the schedule when children can choose to make art. What's different, however, is that you will be specifically encouraging children to express their positive feelings through their creations.

Steps

1. Stock the art center and provide ongoing access to papers, paints, crayons, markers, scissors, collage materials, clays, doughs, and other art materials.
2. Read books to children about how colors and art convey feelings. Some suggestions are *My Many Colored Days* by Dr. Seuss (1996), *How Is Mona Lisa Feeling?* by Julie Merberg (2010), and *Niko Draws a Feeling* by Bob Raczka (2017). Discuss with children how art conveys emotion, exploring the colors and illustrations in the book.
3. Encourage children to create drawings, paintings, collages, and sculptures that tell stories and express their positive feelings.
4. Challenge children to create art that expresses what it's like when they feel good about themselves, when they have solved a problem, had fun, felt happy, or accomplished something that they didn't think they could do. In short, encourage them to translate optimistic feelings into art. If they prefer to explore the materials rather than creating a product, that is perfectly fine.
5. Display the children's signed art in the classroom at a height where the children can see and appreciate the creations. Use colored paper strips, poster board, or inexpensive frames to highlight the work.
6. Have children dictate a description of their art pieces and the feelings they express. Write the statement on a sentence strip (in the child's home language and English) and post underneath the artwork rather than on the art itself.

Example

Obviously art creations are individual to each child. The examples at right exemplify the artists' happiness and optimism. The choice of drawing the sun, flowers, a butterfly, clouds, and heart designs reflect beauty, joy, freedom, and gratitude.

Follow-up

1. Invite children to express their positive emotions through the other arts—dance, movement, and music. What does happiness sound like when played on drums and maracas? What does it look like in dance form?
2. Encourage children to revisit their art. During classroom activities, take the opportunity to point out the children's creations and remind them of the positive, optimistic feelings they convey.

Engaging Families

1. Encourage families to provide art materials and tools—and time and a place to use them—at home. These supplies do not need to be expensive. A few simple items are best. Suggest found and recycled objects that work well, such as paper towel rolls and fabric scraps. If you have a reusable resource center near you (see www.reuseresources.org for a list of centers), collect items to share with families or plan a family field trip so families can choose their own supplies.
2. Give families copies of handout 9 from appendix B so they can do a family version of this activity at home. Post it online too if you have a classroom web page or blog.
3. Create music-and-movement backpacks to place in a lending library. Each backpack can include scarves or long pieces of fabric, rhythm instruments, instructions for making more instruments at home, and a suggestion sheet for how to use the items for self-expression.

" ——————————————————

Encouraging children to build their self-esteem through the visual arts helps to decrease depression and increase optimistic thinking. As an example of one child's art, she drew herself with a smile on her face, the sun shining, and a snowman smiling.

—Shana Andoe, Preschool Teacher

—————————————————— "

" ——————————————————

I formed small groups and asked the children to draw themselves feeling happy or with what makes them feel happy. We've been talking about emotions all school year, so this was an easy task for them. Then they painted their drawings using watercolors.

We read the books *The Dot* and *Ish* (both by Peter H. Reynolds) . . . to encourage positive artistic feelings. After their work dried, I matted and had each child autograph his or her artwork. . . . We hung the paintings over the Promethean Board so everyone could see and discuss our work. Later we moved the art to right outside our classroom, where we will see it every day.

—Cassandra Redding, Head Start Teacher

—————————————————— "

ACTIVITY 11

Display and Discuss Posters with Positive Messages

The items you choose to hang on the walls are not just decorative. Whether they consist of images alone or have accompanying text, they provide opportunities to engage children in learning about optimism.

Steps

1. Choose images and posters that convey positive and optimistic messages. Select anything you think will convey this message to the children, such as a photo of a child sharing a toy, friends jumping in the air in joy, and a nature photo that evokes pleasant emotions. How much print to include depends on children's stages of development.
2. Display one or a few posters in the classroom at children's eye level.
3. Introduce and discuss the posters at group time. Invite children to respond to the images.
4. Use the posters as conversation starters and tie them into daily life as appropriate. Encourage children to point them out to classroom visitors and explain why they think it's good to think optimistically.
5. Invite children to create their own artwork to display as posters. Artwork from activity 10 could become posters.

Example

To give you some ideas, the following images were downloaded from the internet. The Pinterest website (www.pinterest.com) has a wealth of suggestions under "optimism posters for children."

Follow-up

1. Complement the posters by displaying photos that capture optimistic moments for the children in the classroom. Photos might show the children caring for pets, hugging one another, enthusiastically jumping in the air, and comforting friends.
2. Use a sentence strip to label the positivity illustrated in each picture (in children's home languages and English). For example, you might write, "Carlos is showing his friend Jasmine how to mend a book with a torn page" next to a photo of the two children repairing a book.
3. Regularly refer children to the photos of themselves. Discuss how they felt when the photo was taken and how they feel when they look at these photos now. What do these photos tell them about daily life in their classroom? What positive messages can be found in the photos?
4. Acknowledge similarities when someone in the class acts like a child in a photo or poster. Explore with the child whether she feels like the child in the photo/poster and what feeling that might be.

Engaging Families

1. Hold a family workshop for making smaller versions of positive message posters. Invite families to bring photos, magazines, and other items to use in their posters. Provide construction paper (small to medium in size) and other supplies they will need. Families can hang the finished posters at home, in prominent and "surprise" places. For example, they might hang a poster that says "Have a Great Day" on the back of a closet door.

2. Provide a list of simple, positive sayings you use with the children in the classroom. For example, "Mistakes are part of learning" or "Be kind to others." Encourage families to use these sayings at home to reinforce the optimism children are learning in the classroom.

We've had positive emoji posters up in the classroom all year. I introduced them the first day and discussed what they mean and why they are important to all of us. There are times when I remind the children of these positive messages when we meet an obstacle in the classroom or in life.

—Simona Moss, Teacher

ACTIVITY 12

Help Children Reflect on Optimism Daily with the Gratitude Box

In this activity, children learn to be aware of the positive things in their lives. This helps them understand that even though they face problems and obstacles, there is always something good to find and build upon. Martin Seligman calls these memories "good time nuggets." They are especially useful for children who have communication disorders and may have difficulty recalling and retelling the positive events in their lives.

The activity is a form of reflection, which builds gratitude and is closely linked with optimism. By combining the two qualities in one activity, both are reinforced. (Note: This activity is based on an idea from Karen Reivich's 2010 *Fishful Thinking* podcast episode on cultivating optimism: www.blogtalkradio.com /fishfulthinking/2010/05/24/think-positive.)

Steps

1. Make a Gratitude Box. A cardboard boot box is about the right size. Cut a slit in the box top large enough for index cards to be slipped inside. Cover the box with plain paper.

2. Invite the children to decorate the box with crayons or paint, or by gluing on items such as shells, sparkles, and ribbon. Then place the box on a shelf or table within children's reach.

3. Introduce the box to children during a group meeting. Define the word *gratitude*, and describe how the Gratitude Box will be used: Everyone will gather at the Gratitude Box each day at a set time, such as before going home. Explain that you and the children will think about three happy things that took place that day. Let children know that if they need help, you can refresh their memories. You will then help the children record the positive memories on separate index cards. Children can draw a picture, sign their names (or as much of their name as they know), or leave them anonymous. You will also write your own memories to put in the Gratitude Box. Talk while you write so children can hear what happy things happened to you that day. Demonstrate how they will put the completed memory cards into the Gratitude Box.

4. Remind children during the day to pay attention and be on the lookout for the good things that happen. At this age, children tend to be egocentric, so

help them expand their thinking to include others, such as "Shandra was nice to Jan" or "Jenny's mom made yummy bread with us."

5. Open the Gratitude Box either daily or weekly at the morning meeting, depending on your schedule. Reach in, randomly take out one card at a time, and read it aloud. If a memory is signed, ask the author to share why the memory was good and how it made her feel. If memories are anonymous, discuss them as a group. Read as many treasured memories as will hold the children's interest—which may be only a few for younger children.

Example

Memories will be unique to each child and setting. Here are some examples:

1. I threw a ball into a hoop for the first time today. (Matthew)
2. I helped Susie feel better when she fell and scraped her leg. (LaTanya)
3. We had tacos for lunch today. (Anonymous)
4. I was picked to be a helper. (Chinua)
5. Miss Jane took a photo of my block tower, and we made a sign saying, "Please leave this up." (Nevaeh)
6. I did a very hard puzzle. (Graham)
7. Olivia's mom ate lunch with us. (Keisha)
8. Our classroom fish—Mrs. Fish—had babies. She ate some of them, but two of them are alive! (Seth)
9. We had fun singing in the halls. (Dylan)
10. Marcel showed me how to look up something on the computer, even though it took me a while to learn. (Aldona)

Follow-up

Vary the Gratitude Box activity in the following ways.

1. Record memories in journals. If the children already keep daily journals, they can record their three treasured memories by dictating to you. As with the Gratitude Box, these entries can be shared at a group meeting, or they can be kept with each child as a personal record, if preferred.
2. Try writing children's treasured memories in a journal right before rest time so children go to sleep or rest with the pleasant thoughts of what went well on their minds. You might put each child's journal and a pencil or crayon directly on their cot or mat. As you tuck children in, you can go over their journal entries with them. Place the journal under the cot or the side of the mat when you are finished. At group time at the end of the day, children can

share what they thought went well with the full group or keep the journal entries private.

3. Create a Gratitude Bulletin Board in the classroom. With children's permission, post sample index cards and/or invite the children to illustrate them. A possible title for the bulletin board could be "Good Things Are Always Happening Here."

4. Make a Gratitude Book that includes photographs of positive moments and events in the classroom. For example, you could take photographs of children, staff, and family members enjoying a field trip, joking together, or experiencing the first snowfall of the year. Use the photographs to make a book, writing captions under each photo. Display the books in the library area, where children can pick them up whenever they want to relive these moments and the optimistic feelings they evoke.

Engaging Families

1. Invite families to look at the children's gratitude cards and, if you make one, the class gratitude book. Make extra copies of the book so families can take it home and look at it with their children.

2. Provide a copy of handout 10 in appendix B, and suggest that families try this activity at home to reinforce the importance of looking for good things in life. Post it online too if you have a classroom web page or blog.

66

At lunch we ask the children to tell us three positive or happy things that happened during the morning. We write them down, thank the children for sharing their treasured memories, and place them in the Gratitude Box. At the next day's circle time, we choose some to read aloud to the group. This is especially helpful for children who have a hard time separating from their parents in the morning. They now have something to look forward to at the morning circle time.

—Sarah Bollingmo, Preschool Site Supervisor

99

CHAPTER 5

The Optimistic Educator

We need to assume an optimistic view in order for us to feel like we can make a difference in the lives of our children. Furthermore, if we want our children to be resilient and optimistic, we need to model it.

—MARY BETH HEWITT

For children to become optimistic thinkers, they need to be guided by teachers and administrators who value and support the importance of thinking optimistically. Everyone in a child care program, family child care home, or school needs to regard teaching optimism as a vital part of the curriculum and a targeted goal for all. Only when every person in a leadership position is committed to this end will it become attainable. Leading for Children, an organization dedicated to supporting best practices in early childhood leadership, considers optimistic leadership a foundational principle for child success (Jablon, accessed 2018).

In this chapter, we apply content from previous chapters, this time focusing on you as an educator and leader. Having learned about the lifelong benefits of optimism, concepts related to optimism, the role of explanatory style, how to set up an environment to support optimism, and how to encourage and teach young children to become optimistic thinkers, it is time to focus on your own explanatory style.

In most everything you do and say, you are a role model for the children you teach. They notice, listen to, and respond to your behavior, interactions, and mood. If you have a pessimistic response to life events, children will copy this. Children who already use a negative explanatory style will continue this approach to interpreting adversity. Children with a positive approach will start questioning their explanatory style. If, on the other hand, you have an optimistic response and positive explanatory style, then the children will copy that. Children who already use an optimistic explanatory style will have this approach reinforced, while children with a negative explanatory style will start disputing pessimistic thoughts.

If you are already an optimist, you can benefit from enhancing your explanatory style. If you are a pessimist, it's time to change your style. It's definitely worth

> **"**
> What the teacher is, is more important than what he teaches.
>
> —Karl Menninger
> **"**

the effort. Becoming optimistic will make you more effective in your work. Just as it is hard to teach someone to cook if you lack the skills and passion for cooking, it is difficult to teach children optimistic thinking unless you have a positive approach and are passionate about teaching it. And as discussed throughout the book, becoming optimistic will also enhance many aspects of your life.

Optimistic Teachers

Daily life in a typical preschool or kindergarten classroom is filled with challenges. Some are preventable through thoughtful planning and applying knowledge of child development. However, many challenges—such as those caused by weather, family circumstances, or illnesses—are unavoidable. Realistically, teachers who have a positive explanatory style tend to have an easier time overcoming adversity and handling challenges as they occur. Consider how two different teachers respond to the following situation.

Some preschoolers are getting ready to go outdoors to play. It's sunny, but the temperature is cooler than yesterday. The children put on their coats, hats, and mittens. Lyla puts on her coat and hat, then realizes her mittens are at home. And wouldn't you know it—the box of extra winter clothing is missing.

In chapter 2, we discussed the Three Ps of explanatory style. If Lyla's teacher is a pessimistic educator with a negative explanatory style, her response might be like this:

- **Personal:** I should have noticed that Lyla didn't arrive with her mittens. I usually have extra scarves and mittens on hand, but I don't know where they are. I am so disorganized.
- **Pervasive:** Lyla can't go outdoors without her mittens, but she also can't stay indoors by herself. That means nobody will be able to go out—nobody will get the exercise they need. Everyone will have trouble focusing and getting along with each other this afternoon.
- **Permanent:** The director will ask me why the class didn't go outdoors. I'll have to explain why I don't have extra mittens on hand. She'll realize I'm disorganized, and she'll notice all my other faults too.

The pessimistic educator blames herself for Lyla not having her mittens, turns the minor challenge affecting one child into something that affects the entire class, and worries that this will make her director pay closer attention to everything she does. Her response leads to poor practice as none of the children get to go outdoors and enjoy playing on a sunny day.

However, if Lyla's teacher is an optimistic educator with a positive explanatory style, her response might be like this:

- **Personal:** It's typical for children and families to forget a hat or mittens this time of year, when the weather is warm one day and cool the next. I must have misplaced the box of extra items.
- **Pervasive:** Lyla can wear my gloves today. They will be a little big, but they will stay on her hands and keep her warm. I can go without gloves for one day.
- **Permanent:** Today I'll send home a reminder note asking families to be sure their children have the clothing they need to have fun playing outdoors in all kinds of weather. I'll look for the box of extra items too so we'll have them on hand for the next time someone forgets their hat or mittens.

The optimistic educator recognizes the situation is confined to this one particular event. She thinks of short- and long-term solutions: Lyla can wear her gloves, she will look for the box of extra items, and she will send home a reminder note.

As explained in chapter 2, learned optimism relies on accurate, nonnegative thinking. This means that although you can respond to a situation in terms of its permanence, pervasiveness, and personal causation, an optimistic explanatory style does not have to be 100 percent positive. Realism is important, and a negative belief might be appropriate, given the facts. Positive beliefs must be well founded and based on evidence. In the previous example, the optimistic teacher believes that she must have misplaced the box of extra scarves and mittens. Her optimistic response acknowledges both her responsibility for misplacing the box and her plans to look for it.

According to Martin Seligman (2006), for most optimists there are times when they are rightly pessimistic. He recommends the following: Use optimism when you are focused on achievement, concerned about feelings, experiencing a long-term health concern, or leading and inspiring others. Use pessimism when you're planning for a risky and uncertain future, counseling others whose future is dim, and offering sympathy (optimism can come later).

When faced with a challenging situation, it's important to consider the likely risks and outcomes. If the risk is relatively low—frustration, loss of time, feeling upset—optimism is a useful response. If the risk is high—having an accident, losing one's home, becoming seriously ill—pessimism based on real evidence is most likely the effective response.

Determining Your Explanatory Style

To examine and understand your explanatory style, you can begin by taking the test suggested in chapter 1. But to get further insight into what the results mean, use the ABCDE approach on yourself, much as you do with children. To begin, Seligman suggests keeping an ABC journal for one to two days. Each time you experience adversity (A), describe what happened using just the facts—similar to an objective observation record. Next, record your beliefs (B)—how you interpreted the situation. Finally, write down the consequences (C)—how you felt and what you did in response. The goal of this exercise is to focus on your explanatory style. Later you can address it through disputation (D) and energization (E).

Here are two sample journal entries demonstrating how different teachers—one who uses pessimistic thinking and one who uses optimistic thinking—might respond to adversity (A). In this scenario, the adversity (A) is the same for both teachers, but their beliefs (B) and thus their consequences (C) differ.

Teacher 1 uses pessimistic thinking:

- **Adversity (A):** This morning, Derek's mom brought him to the classroom. I said, "Good morning, Derek. Would you like to show your mom the baby bunnies?" His mom said, "I'm in a hurry. He can show me another time." She hurried down the hall to the front door. I walked Derek to the bunnies, and we watched them nurse for a while.
- **Beliefs (B):** I know Derek's mom was in a hurry, but yesterday he was excited about the babies and talked about having me show them to her. She is late at least once a week. Why can't she plan her morning so she has time for a brief visit?
- **Consequences (C):** When Derek and his mother arrived the next day, I made sure I was busy with something else. I was afraid I might tell her what was on my mind.

Teacher 2 uses optimistic thinking:

- **Adversity (A):** This morning, Derek's mom brought him to the classroom. I said, "Good morning, Derek. Would you like to show your mom the baby bunnies?" His mom said, "I'm in a hurry. He can show me another time." She hurried down the hall to the front door. I walked Derek to the bunnies, and we watched them nurse for a while.
- **Beliefs (B):** I know Derek's mom is frequently in a hurry. I wonder if something is happening at home or work to cause her stress. What can I do to be supportive—of her and of Derek?

- **Consequences (C):** I posted photos of the baby bunnies on our class website. When Derek and his mother arrived the next day, I suggested they look at them at home together when they had time. I also asked privately if everything is okay. She said she has a new boss and needs to make a good impression by being on time.

After you have recorded five journal entries about your own teaching challenges, review them while avoiding judging yourself. The goal is to see how your beliefs (B) are linked to the consequences (C). You will find that pessimistic beliefs tend to lead to passive consequences, such as avoiding Derek and his mother—which is both unprofessional and inappropriate. Optimistic beliefs are followed by energetic consequences, such as posting the baby bunny photos on the class website—a teaching practice that benefits all the children and families.

It's not necessary to continue using an ABC journal after this initial exercise. But if you find it helpful, it can be a useful tool for staying aware of and dealing with a pessimistic explanatory style. When you're short on time, it can also be helpful to make quick notes about your thoughts when they occur. You can then set a time when you will be free to review your notes and focus on how you will counter pessimistic thoughts.

If you do decide to keep an ABC journal while identifying your explanatory style, later you can add two more categories—disputation (D) and energization (E)—to document the full ABCDE model.

Countering Pessimistic Thoughts with Distraction and Disputation

If you determine that you have a pessimistic explanatory style, there are two simple ways to counteract negative thoughts: distraction, a short-term approach, and disputation, a more effective and longer-lasting strategy you are already familiar with. You can effectively use distraction and disputation in tandem. You don't have to pick one technique over the other.

Distraction uses physical techniques to draw attention to your pessimistic thoughts so you become aware of them and can then stop them. Listed below are some of the techniques that other educators have found useful that can be easily used in a classroom or family child care home. These are not meant to be used by children. When you have pessimistic thoughts, try out these distraction techniques on yourself:

- Write *STOP* in large letters on an index card. Put it in your pocket so it's easy to take out and read.

- Place a rubber band on your wrist. Snap it or move it to the other wrist.
- Put a drop of lotion in your hands and rub them together.
- Carry a small, smooth object—such as a shell, marble, or stone—in your pocket. Hold it and rub it with your thumb.

Disputation (D), as you are aware of from the ABCDE model, involves challenging your pessimistic thoughts. To dispute your thinking effectively, you must use facts to refute your beliefs (B). You're not trying to fool yourself into thinking optimistically. You want to convince yourself that your initial beliefs were based on faulty conclusions.

Let's look at how both distraction and disputation might work in practice. Janis, an early childhood coach, follows a predetermined schedule for visiting classrooms. After each visit, she sends the classroom team an email to summarize their conversations, outline the next steps everyone agreed to, and remind them of their next appointment.

Today when Janis arrives for her scheduled visit to the Friendly Frogs room, the children are getting ready for a storytelling visit from the children's librarian. The librarian's visit was rescheduled from last month when she had been sick. The teachers had forgotten to tell Janis about the change.

The plan for Janis's visit, as discussed and recorded via email, had been for her to model a small-group math activity focused on geometric shapes. Janis had spent considerable time gathering materials and planning the activity. While the children seem excited about the librarian's visit, Janis is quite upset.

Janis's first response to the situation includes negative explanatory thoughts:

- **Permanent:** These teachers are never going to learn how to teach math, and it will be my fault.
- **Pervasive:** This kind of thing happens all the time. I expect too much from teachers.
- **Personal:** I am not a good coach for these teachers. I should have reminded them about the math activity.

But because Janis is working on changing her explanatory style, she reaches for the *STOP* card in her pocket. She doesn't need to take it out—just touching it is enough to distract her thinking.

Janis takes a deep breath and tells herself, "I'll think this over later, at my desk. I can make some tea and review what happened and what I thought in response. I'm not going to tell the teachers now how disappointed I am." In the meantime, she sits with the children, trying to enjoy the librarian's visit. She hopes to learn something about storytelling.

Later, while sipping her tea, a calmer Janis recognizes how the distraction technique helped her avoid a potentially inappropriate consequence (*C*) of complaining to the teachers. Next she takes time to dispute (*D*) her beliefs (*B*) with these facts:

- **Permanent:** These teachers already know a lot about teaching math. They have a wonderful math center and make engaging math games. They asked for help with geometry, so that's why I had planned an activity. I can discuss with the teachers when would be a good time to reschedule the geometry activity.
- **Pervasive:** Schedule snafus are rare, in part because I do send follow-up emails as reminders. The teachers never say that I ask too much of them.
- **Personal:** I get positive reviews from the teachers I coach and from my supervisor. Everyone can improve, but I am already doing a good job. The teachers just forgot to tell me about the schedule change.

Having disputed (*D*) her pessimistic beliefs (*B*), Janis can now add the energization (*E*) element. She tells herself, "It's not a big deal. I can do the geometry activity next week. And as it turned out, I learned some new strategies for storytelling."

Be Alert for Thinking Traps

In chapter 2, we introduced the concept of thinking traps: the tendency to use mental shortcuts to process information (Reivich and Shatté 2002; Pearson and Hall 2017). Thinking traps make it difficult to use accurate and flexible thinking—the kind of thinking needed for an optimistic explanatory style. They affect both children and adults.

The chart on page 102 provides thinking trap examples relevant for educators. You can use this as a guide to help you notice and avoid your own thinking traps.

Thinking Trap	Description	Example	Reality
Jumping to conclusions	Assuming something is true based on little or no evidence.	"Today Jason couldn't throw the ball back to Seth. Jason must have physical delays."	Seth was joking with Jason. He stepped farther and farther away until Jason couldn't throw the ball far enough to reach him.
Mind reading	Assuming we know another person's thoughts; expecting another person to know what we are thinking.	"Our director knows I always take off the day after Thanksgiving. I guess she doesn't want me to do that this year, because she put me on the schedule for Friday."	A new staff member made the schedule this year. She doesn't know what this teacher has done in the past.
Emotional reasoning	Drawing a conclusion based on feelings or intuition rather than fact.	"I should be able to do this, but I'm not a creative person. Someone else will have to redesign our music and movement center."	This teacher is quite creative but does not recognize her talents.
Overgeneralizing	Making an assumption about someone or something based on only one or two experiences.	"My coteacher never helps the children get their cots out at naptime. She is always avoiding this task."	One time the coteacher was unavailable to help with the cots because she was helping a child pick up some beads spilled on the floor.
Magnifying/Minimizing	Overemphasizing negative events and seeing positive events as unimportant; making too much of positive events and ignoring the negative.	"Look at all of the food under the table. These children are too young to serve themselves."	Only one child had difficulty; she is still learning to use the large serving spoons.
Catastrophizing	Assuming that the worst-case scenario is in place; exaggerating the likelihood that something bad will happen or exaggerating how bad it will be.	"I know the children enjoy taking field trips, but so many things can go wrong. What if it rains at the zoo or we lose someone?"	The program has a planning process for field trips to prepare for contingencies. The weather report says it will be sunny all day.

Apply Positive Skills to Your Personal and Professional Life

In chapter 1, we outlined positive skills related to optimism: resilience, mindfulness, growth mindset, grit, gratitude, happiness, and kindness. Often these serve as precursors or complements to optimistic thinking. Below are suggestions educators can use to build these skills in themselves to support the development of their optimistic explanatory style.

Resilience

Resilient teachers can bounce back from adversity and continue to enjoy life and pursue meaningful goals. Try developing and applying these seven critical abilities to boost your resilience (Reivich and Shatté 2002):

1. **Stay calm under pressure and express emotions in a helpful way (emotional regulation):** "I am so sorry your child got hurt. I can go over the accident report now, or if you prefer, we can do it later."

2. **Delay gratification and follow through on goals (impulse control):** "Those tomatoes look delicious, but they are not quite ripe. Tomorrow they will be perfect."

3. **Analyze the causes of problems (causal analysis):** "The children don't want to pick up before lunch because they are still working. Let's think about a different approach to cleanup time."

4. **Understand the needs and feelings of others (empathy):** "I think some of the children are so hungry at arrival that they are not ready to play. We can have a self-serve breakfast ready for them."

5. **Stay positive while accepting reality (optimism):** "I know children are expected to know their letters in kindergarten, but worksheets are not developmentally appropriate. We can find other ways to help them make progress toward gaining this skill."

6. **Believe they can persevere and solve problems (self-efficacy):** "There's no money in the budget for a printer. I'll put out the word to the community that we need one and see if someone can help."

7. **Take on new opportunities and connect with others (reaching out):** "I signed up for an online early childhood book club. At a getting-to-know-you meeting, we will choose the first book."

Mindfulness

Mindful teachers use all their senses to focus on the children, what they are doing and learning, and what they need. The strategies used for teaching mindfulness to young children can help educators too.

- **Use breaks to give yourself time for quiet and relaxation—in the present.** Try to free your mind from revisiting what took place in the classroom before your break and what might happen after it.
- **Use your senses to pay attention to the world around you.** You will be benefiting yourself and modeling for the children.
- **Pay attention to your own breathing while leading children in a breathing activity.** You will feel as calm and refreshed as the children.

- **Convey caring wishes to others.** Being kind to others makes you feel good about yourself.
- **Focus on gratitude every day.** As you fall asleep, think about the day and reflect on things for which you are grateful.

Growth Mindset

Your mindset is the way you think about your own traits and abilities. Those with a fixed mindset think they can't change what they were born with and that there is no point in trying. Those with a growth mindset, on the other hand, believe that hard work and perseverance help them achieve goals.

Teachers' mindsets affect their expectations for children. Negative assumptions about a child's ability to learn can hamper the child's progress. The same is true for you. If you have a fixed mindset about your abilities, you will not be able to take on new challenges, such as developing an optimistic explanatory style.

You can help yourself build a growth mindset in much the same way that you help children do this (Lift Education 2017):

- Keep in mind that the brain grows throughout life and that new skills are gained through hard work, determination, and practice.
- Focus on what you have learned in life, not what you still do not know. Reflect on new learning, and plan ways to apply it.
- Congratulate yourself when you feel confident enough to try something new.
- See mistakes as signs of progress, not signs you have failed.
- Learn with someone. Take a class or ask a friend to be your partner in gaining knowledge or developing a new skill.
- Take your time. Learning does not have to be on a fast track. Enjoy the learning process.
- Accept challenges that come your way, especially those that are out of your comfort zone.

Grit

People with grit have a passion for long-term goals and the perseverance needed to achieve them. They also have a growth mindset, know their abilities, believe their actions lead to certain outcomes, and are optimistic.

Let's examine how one teacher developed grit. Preschool teacher Selena Okoye thinks, "Next year Josie, a child with cerebral palsy, will be in my class. I want to be fully prepared to support her development and learning and partner with her family. I've never taken an online course, but I've found one that will help me prepare for this new challenge."

Selena used several strategies to develop grit.

- She gave herself credit for what she had already done on the way to achieving a personal goal. "I visited a lot of websites and read articles about cerebral palsy. Now I know what I still need to learn."
- She spent time with people who model the behaviors and attitudes needed to remain focused on a goal. "In the online class, my fellow students are learning with me and sharing their ideas and experiences."
- She was flexible, seeing obstacles and problems as opportunities to grow and learn. "I need to observe the teachers in a program that has a child with cerebral palsy enrolled."
- She set small goals to reach on the way to achieving her larger goal. "To learn about the causes, symptoms, and medical treatment options for cerebral palsy, I read and took notes on a few pages a day."
- She built time into the day for open-minded, supportive reflection. "I feel ready to meet Josie and her family. Together we'll plan how to create an inclusive environment that allows Josie to thrive and learn."

Gratitude

Gratitude is thankful appreciation for what we have received. Grateful people focus on what they have—not what they lack. To cultivate gratitude, teachers can do the following (Harvard Medical School 2011):

- **Write a thank-you note.** Thank a child, a family, a colleague, or a volunteer. You could thank all the families in an email or through a notice in the class newsletter.
- **Think about why you are grateful for others.** Share your thoughts with a colleague or the children. "I enjoyed our gathering when each of you described what you did at choice time."
- **Keep a gratitude journal.** This gives you something to share with loved ones and to look back on in the future.
- **Count your blessings.** Once a week, review your experiences and record what went well or what was particularly wonderful.
- **Pray.** Teachers who are religious find it helpful to use prayer to cultivate gratitude.
- **Meditate.** Focus on why you chose to become an educator and what you appreciate about working with children and families.

Happiness

Authentic happiness includes optimism. Review the happiness-enhancing strategies in chapter 1, and try the following strategies (Busch 2016):

- **Focus on feelings in the present.** Teaching involves a lot of planning, but it's best to value the present and not be overly concerned about the future. "Today was a great day. We played music while the children painted, and they were even more creative than usual."
- **Connect with people.** Teachers often work in teams, which means they have ready-made partners in the classroom and program. "Good morning, Mr. Colin. Do you have photos of the new baby? I'd love to see them."
- **Be kind to others.** Try being especially kind to children, families, and colleagues. "Dionne, I'm glad I caught you. Here's a copy of the recipe you asked for at our potluck lunch."
- **Invest in experiences, not possessions.** Possessions do not bring people joy, but experiences can create memories that last a lifetime. Treat yourself to interesting and engaging experiences. "My partner and I love live shows. We got tickets to see a play next month."
- **Embrace your bad moods.** Sometimes there are good reasons for feeling out of sorts. Try to pinpoint the cause and learn from your feelings. "My son left for basic training. I miss him a lot."
- **Get outside.** Think of outdoor play times as opportunities for you to enjoy a different setting and appreciate your surroundings. "Who wants to run with me? Sarah, Jocelyn, Marco—will you join me?"

Kindness

Kind people are warmhearted, considerate, humane, and sympathetic. Their kind acts can be spontaneous or planned. We learn to be kind when others are kind to us and by practicing kindness.

As members of a caring profession, teachers spend their days being kind to others, especially children. Sometimes children express feelings and frustration in inappropriate ways, and we don't feel kind toward them. Yet these are precisely the children who will benefit the most from kindness. Every child, family member, colleague, and supervisor deserves your kindness.

During a typical day, an educator might perform the following acts of kindness:

- comforting a child who misses his mother
- telling a father about something wonderful his child did that day
- bringing flowers from her garden for a colleague

- paying attention to her own physical and emotional well-being as well as that of the children

You increase your optimism by being resilient and mindful, by having a growth mindset and grit, and by expressing gratitude, happiness, and kindness. At the same time, you can become an optimistic role model to the children you teach by altering your pessimistic thinking with the same ABCDE process that you use to help them change their negative explanatory styles. Moreover, by striving to become more optimistic, you will reap the many health, professional, and personal benefits of optimism detailed in chapter 1.

Optimistic Leaders

Most, if not all, staff in a high-quality early childhood setting play some type of leadership role in their program. Some staff work directly with children and families, while others supervise staff, plan and monitor budgets, report to funders, and perform myriad tasks that ensure the program is effective and excellent.

Teachers lead children, colleagues, and families. They might guide family members who are organizing a parenting book club, model developmentally appropriate practice for teaching assistants, and, of course, foster children's play and learning—often by following the children's lead.

Other staff and consultants are also leaders as they contribute to enhancing children's development and learning. These individuals might be coaches or specialists for health, nutrition, mental health, disabilities, social services, and family engagement.

The leadership contributions of all staff are vital to the program's success. Typically, however, an early childhood setting has a designated primary leader. This individual has a specific title—principal, director, administrator, and so on—and responsibilities for operating all parts of the program.

While this book addresses learned optimism for children and teachers, we now wish to direct our attention to the primary leaders in early childhood education settings. Any focus on learned optimism needs the full support of the principal or director and should be built in to coaching and other professional development strategies. Information about learned optimism might bubble up from the experiences of one or more teachers or a mental health specialist, or it could be introduced by a director or principal who believes it is a worthy addition to the curriculum. Regardless, all staff should take part in planning, implementing, evaluating, and enhancing a learned optimism initiative.

> " Optimistic leaders focus on opportunities. Optimism is magnetic. Optimism enables open-mindedness, and open-mindedness enables collaboration, creativity, and problem solving. . . . Oh, and did I mention that optimists enjoy their work more and have a lot more fun?
>
> —Bert Jacobs, Chief Executive Optimist, the Life is Good Kids Foundation

Characteristics of Optimistic Leaders

1. They look for solutions.
2. They are not afraid to make mistakes or even to fail.
3. They are clear and effective communicators.
4. They think about the future.
5. They use language to motivate others.
6. Their behavior is infectious.
7. They value collaboration.
8. They have a success mindset.

(Adapted from "8 Reasons Why Optimists Are Better Leaders" by Kathryn Sandford)

Setting the Tone for Optimism

Directors, principals, coaches, and other early childhood leaders set the tone for an optimistic workplace through their core beliefs, everyday practices, and interactions. It's not just teachers who need to model the use of optimistic thinking to children. All leaders need to model their own optimistic approach for their staff. Following are examples of how optimistic leaders can foster an optimistic early childhood work setting.

Believe That Mistakes Are Inevitable and Valuable Opportunities for Learning

Ms. Kay is the director of the Learning to Learn Pre-K Program. In her office hangs a hand-embroidered sign saying, "Assume the best." This is a core belief that underlies her interactions with staff.

For example, during a classroom visit, she finds several children seated on the floor by their cubbies, removing wet socks and replacing them with dry ones. She calmly asks Ms. Juno, the teacher, "What happened here?" Before Ms. Juno can respond, Ms. Kay adds, "And how can I help?"

It turns out that a spill at the water table turned into a creative child's science experiment: "What will happen if we mop up the water with our feet?" Before the teachers could intervene, Emily, the "scientist," had involved several friends in the activity.

Ms. Kay offers to take over story time while Ms. Juno finishes cleaning up with Emily and another child who volunteers to help. Later Ms. Kay helps Ms. Juno reflect on what caused the initial spill. Ms. Juno realizes that it would be best to reduce the number of children who can use the water table at one time. This would reduce spills. As for the preschool scientist, she plans to channel Emily's enthusiasm into other, less chaotic science explorations.

Recognize, Acknowledge, and Build on Strengths

Although not clearly visible in the above example of optimistic leadership, Ms. Kay's response was guided by recognizing, acknowledging, and building on strengths. When she saw the children replacing their wet socks with dry ones, she did not intervene. She knew they could do this task on their own, and she valued the children's ability to develop independence.

She also knew Ms. Juno, a teacher skilled at keeping an organized classroom, could get it back in order—with a little help. Knowing that she herself was a skilled and charming storyteller, Ms. Kay offered to take over the daily read-aloud. And Ms. Juno, recognizing Emily's creativity and interest in scientific concepts, planned ways to build on this strength during future experiences.

Using a strength-building approach similar to the one she and Ms. Kay used with children, Ms. Juno engaged family volunteers for the preschool's annual outdoor spring cleanup day. First, she and a group of teachers created a list of the jobs and associated skills needed for the event to be successful. To illustrate, they needed a parent with organizational and play skills to plan games and activities and to care for the children in attendance; a creative meal planner to organize lunch and snacks; and leaders who could use tools and follow plans for the building and repair crews. Parents signed up for the jobs that were a good match for their own skills and experience. Thanks to this process, the volunteers felt proud of their work and saw the value of their efforts and accomplishments.

Celebrate Efforts, Progress, and Accomplishments

At the beginning of the school year, Mr. Hartmann, team leader for the kindergarten classes at the Lake Street Elementary School, suggests that his fellow kindergarten teachers set a goal for enhancing something about their practice and developing a plan for achieving the goal. One experienced kindergarten teacher has observed that today's children start school with less-developed fine-motor skills than in the past. She's read that this is due, in part, to the amount of time children spend using digital devices. She sets a goal to embed in the curriculum numerous opportunities for children to naturally build and use their fine-motor skills throughout the day.

As a first step, she keeps track of everything the children do during the day, from stowing their belongings in their cubbies to reading books. She notes how the children use fine-motor skills to perform these tasks and activities. Mr. Hartmann checks in with this teacher and learns that she has now moved on to the next step in her plan: determining ways to incorporate fine-motor building as part of the day's routines and activities.

Mr. Hartmann celebrates this teacher's progress and accomplishments. He says, "Congratulations on completing your first step and starting on the second one. You noticed all the different ways children could be developing this skill if they were encouraged to do so. Like a researcher, you defined the baseline—how the children already use fine-motor skills—and now you are planning ways to enhance their use."

Show Gratitude

The Learning to Learn Pre-K Program is developing its annual budget. Ms. Kay, the director, has collected information from the teachers—what they need and what they wish for to keep their classrooms engaging. She thinks, "These teachers are so dedicated and so effective, I want to thank them in a concrete way. Salaries are set by the local education agency, but I can include funds in next year's budget for small cash awards for extraordinary performance. Extra compensation will convey how much the program values on-the-job excellence." She adds a professional gratitude line to the budget.

Focus on the Big Stuff; Don't Sweat the Small Stuff

Let's consider an example where a leader saw the big picture with help from teachers. A preschool teaching team observes that the children seem tired of the materials and experiences in the art center. Having read about the art children create at schools in Reggio Emilia, Italy, they reimagine their art area as a studio stocked with a variety of interesting materials and tools at different stations for painting, drawing, using mirrors, sculpting, tinkering, and reflecting light. They will arrange the center so children can work on their creations with their fellow artists for multiple days at a time. They shut down the current art center for a few days to implement their plans. When they reopen the center as an art studio, they lead tours for the children in small groups.

Not long after the reopening, their coach visits the classroom. "This art center looks much tidier than before," she says in a perfunctory tone. She then proceeds with a planned observation in the literacy area.

The teachers are surprised by the comment. They usually find their coach to be very supportive. When meeting with her later, they share their reactions.

"We worked hard to transform the art center into a studio that would better engage children," they explain. "Yes, it is more organized now, but we have done so much more. Did you notice the other changes we made to better support children's creativity and problem solving?"

The coach apologizes. "I am sorry to have focused on such a small part of your new art center. You're right; the entire center is well thought out and will boost the children's creativity. Can you conduct some observations and take some photos of children using the area to document the children's work? We can discuss them at our next meeting."

The teachers agree, as they too are eager to document how the children use the center and what they are learning in the newly configured space.

Stay in the Moment

Ms. Kay is in her office doing administrative tasks. She looks out the window and sees the rain has cleared. Now there is a beautiful full-arch rainbow in the sky. She leaves her paperwork for later and hurries down the hall to urge the teachers to take the children out to see the rainbow, even though it's lunchtime. "Let's take a few minutes break from lunch," she says. "Hurry outside now so you can see the rainbow."

It takes a minute for the teachers to switch gears, but soon everyone is outdoors oohing and aahing at the beautiful colors in the sky. After they go back inside, the children and teachers talk about the rainbow while finishing lunch. Later, after naps, the children write and illustrate a group story about the day the rainbow came to Learning to Learn. They post the story on the program website so families can read it too.

Create a Physical and Emotional Environment That Supports Optimism

High-quality early childhood settings are safe, healthy, well stocked, and staffed with professionals who enjoy and value their work. Beyond that, however, principals, directors, and other leaders can take additional steps to ensure the environment can support optimism. Here are a few examples of simple but highly effective practices:

- **Do yoga or other mindfulness exercises on-site.** These exercises reduce stress, calm users, and sharpen focus. Schedule a yoga teacher to work with children in the afternoon, near the end of the day. Then have the instructor stay on to lead a staff yoga session. Designate a place where adults can do yoga or meditate on their breaks or before and after work.

- **Institute gratitude rituals.** As a team, decide how, where, and when to express gratitude to each other. You might incorporate it in a class routine, create a gratitude bulletin board where people leave notes for each other, or use a gratitude mailbox to send private notes. Supervisors can consider adding gratitude expressions to the staff meeting agenda.

- **Create an inclusive setting.** Create a space for families, with adult-size chairs. Make accommodations for those with disabilities. Give written and verbal communications in the languages the children, families, and staff speak. Designate areas—away from the children—where staff can take a break, make phone calls, meet with specialists, or respond to parents' emails. Post samples of children's work and photos of them engaged in play. Paint the walls of hallways, conference areas, and staff rooms in colors that appeal to those who will be using these spaces. Post wall decorations that reflect families' cultures, homelands, languages, and interests.

For all early childhood educators, implementing the practices described throughout this chapter will support your professional growth. But to be truly successful, you need to go beyond what is written here. You need to fully understand how optimism benefits children, families, colleagues, team members, and yourself. Teaching optimism requires passionate, optimistic leadership.

Children's Books with Optimistic Themes

One of the most effective ways to support optimism is to stock your program with fiction and nonfiction books focused on handling challenges in positive ways and building skills that support optimistic thinking. The topics, characters, and plots in such books can foster engaging conversations and learning for individuals and groups of children. Here are some suggestions for books for preschoolers and kindergartners.

To find additional books that promote optimism and positivity, the following web pages offer hundreds of choices to consider. You will never run out of wonderful books that encourage children to be optimistic.

- www.positivelypositive.com/2012/05/17/50-top-childrens-books -with-a-positive-message
- www.positivelypositive.com/2013/01/30/50-inspiring-childrens -books-with-a-positive-message-part-2

Fiction

Ada Twist, Scientist by Andrea Beaty. 2016. New York: Abrams Books for Young Readers.
Ada is curious and passionate about science. She perseveres in her efforts to figure out the world.

The Big Orange Splot by Daniel Manus Pinkwater. 1977. New York: Scholastic.
After a big orange splot of paint lands on Mr. Plumbeans's house, he has nonconforming, optimistic dreams of how to redecorate.

Bluebird by Lindsey Yankey. 2014. Vancouver, BC: Simply Read Books.
Little Bluebird is used to flying with help from her friend the wind. When the wind goes missing, she is afraid she won't be able to fly. She frantically searches out the wind only to find that she's been flying on her own.

Bully by Laura Vaccaro Seeger. 2013. New York: Roaring Brook Press.

Bully is a bull, and unfortunately both bullied and a bully himself. After a mean older bull tells him to go away, he acts out and tells his friend the skunk, "You stink!" Eventually Bully faces up to and changes his mean ways.

Charlotte and the Quiet Place by Deborah Sosin. 2015. Berkeley, CA: Plum Blossom Books.

Charlotte loves quiet, but everywhere she goes there is noise from her dog, sirens, swings, and other children. She yearns for a place free of creaks, squeaks, and yapping. Finally she finds a quiet place where she can be calm, compose herself, and breathe deeply.

Chip the Little Computer by Dr. Hope. 1999. Fallbrook, CA: Alpine Publishing.

Chip personifies the values of perseverance and optimism in fulfilling his dream of teaching children to learn. Available in English and Spanish.

Chocolate Milk, Por Favor: Celebrating Diversity with Empathy by Maria Dismondy 2015. Wixom, MI: Cardinal Rule Press.

Gabe, who comes from Brazil, speaks Portuguese. Johnny, a classmate at his new school, is not happy to have Gabe join the class. Through their shared love of soccer, the boys learn to communicate and appreciate each other.

Daydreamers by Tom Feelings and Eloise Greenfield. 1981. New York: Dial Books for Young Readers.

The poetic voices of young African American children are heard through daydreams of hope and optimism. This was the very first book featured on the PBS Kids' TV show *Reading Rainbow*.

The Dot by Peter H. Reynolds. 2003. Somerville, MA: Candlewick Press.

A wise and thoughtful teacher inspires a child who says, "I can't draw," to express her ideas and feelings in imaginative ways.

The Energy Bus for Kids: A Story about Staying Positive and Overcoming Challenges by Jon Gordon. 2012. Hoboken, NJ: Wiley.

Joy the bus driver is able to turn around George's bad day by showing him how a positive attitude can overcome any challenge.

Everyone Can Learn to Ride a Bicycle by Chris Raschka. 2013. New York: Schwartz & Wade.

For many children, learning to ride a bike is a huge accomplishment and a mark of independence. This book outlines the steps in choosing and then learning to ride a bike—from using training wheels to removing the training wheels to riding solo.

Girl, You Are Magic! by Ashley Aya Ferguson. 2018. Tinley Park, IL: Copy & Content Boutique.

Especially powerful for girls, this book is in the form of an inspirational poem. The text focuses on identifying and believing in one's unique abilities.

Glad Monster, Sad Monster by Ed Emberley and Anne Miranda. 1997. New York: LB Kids. Revised edition.

Brightly colored monsters act out different emotions in this book. The text will help children name, identify, and handle their feelings.

Good News Bad News by Jeff Mack. 2012. San Francisco: Chronicle Books.

Using only the four words of the title as text, the adventures of good friends optimistic Rabbit and pessimistic Mouse are explored through their contrasting dispositions.

Happiness Is a Choice by Suzy Liebermann. 2015. Fort Lauderdale: Happy Language Kids.

On the island of Optimism, Hugo the Starfish finds that true happiness begins with optimism.

Howard B. Wigglebottom Learns to Listen by Howard Binkow. 2006. Minneapolis: Lerner.

Howard is a distracted rabbit who has trouble listening. His teacher and friends find this behavior annoying. He realizes he must change and learn to pay attention.

The Hyena Who Lost Her Laugh: A Story about Changing Your Negative Thinking by Jessica Lamb-Shapiro. 2001. Austin: Childswork/Childsplay.

Hillary the Hyena learns that by thinking optimistically, life is better and she can restore her lost laugh.

I Can Do It Myself! by Diane Adams. 2013. Atlanta: Peachtree Publishers.

Emily Pearl can do many things on her own. She can tie her shoes, spread peanut butter, and draw a picture, telling her mother, "I can do it myself!" There comes a time, however, when Emily Pearl needs to ask for help and finds it comforting to have support.

Justine, We're Late!; *Give It Back!*; and *No, It's Mine!* (series on teaching conflict management to children) by Shimrit Nothman. 2014. Self-Published, Amazon Digital Services, Kindle.

Written by a professional conflict negotiator, these three books focus on the same characters, Benjy and Justine, who must figure out how to handle their disagreements.

Last Stop on Market Street by Matt de la Peña. 2015. New York: G. P. Putnam's Sons.

This multi-award-winning book (both Caldecott and Newbery Awards for 2016, among others) tells the story of a boy and his grandmother taking the bus home after church services one Sunday. While the boy sees only negativity—they have no car, the neighborhoods are run-down—his grand-mother looks at the same things and sees only beauty and positivity.

The Little Engine That Could by Watty Piper. (1930) 2005. New York: Philomel.
This classic book, familiar to generations of children, is the quintessential story of the value of optimism. Encourage children to join in with the little train as he says, "I think I can," again and again. Some would contend that the book is a metaphor for the American dream.

McElligot's Pool by Dr. Seuss. 1947. New York: Random House.
This over seventy-year-old classic proves that a child's optimism can't be stopped by adult cynicism.

Mouse Was Mad by Linda Urban. 2012. Orlando, FL: Harcourt Children's Books.
Mouse's friends get mad in different ways—stomping, hopping, and scream-ing. Mouse wants to express his feelings in a way that works for him, is appro-priate, and helps him calm down: being still and quiet.

My Mouth Is a Volcano by Julia Cook. 2006. Chattanooga, TN: National Center for Youth Issues.
Louis has very important thoughts, and sometimes they come out so fast that he interrupts other people. This book can help children learn to respect and listen to others while waiting for their turn to talk.

Pass It On by Sophy Henn. 2017. New York: Philomel.
This upbeat book highlights the power of being grateful and kind by passing on those feelings to others. "When you see something terrific, smile a smile and pass it on! If you chance upon a chuckle, hee hee hee and pass it on. Should you spot a thing of wonder, jump for joy and pass it on!"

Pete the Cat and His Magic Sunglasses by Kimberly and James Dean. 2013. New York: HarperCollins.
It takes a pair of magic sunglasses for Pete to realize there's an optimistic mood inside of him—with or without the glasses.

Rain! by Linda Ashman. 2014. New York: Houghton Mifflin Books for Children.
When rain comes to town, an optimistic young boy is able to change a grumpy old man's attitude.

Rosie Revere, Engineer by Andrea Beaty. 2013. New York: Abrams Books for Young Readers.
Quiet by day, Rosie is a brilliant inventor at night. To help her aunt reach her goal of flying, Rosie builds a flying contraption. It doesn't work, but her aunt encourages her to keep going in the face of failure.

Sink or Swim by Valerie Coulman. (2003) 2017. Self-published (Originally pub-lished in Canada by Lobster Press).

This book reprises Ralph the Cow's role as the quintessential optimist who won't let a little thing like being a cow limit his possibilities.

Spin by Rebecca Janni. 2017. New York: Grosset & Dunlap.

Through the metaphor of persevering on a bike ride through the hills and valleys of life, we learn that we can reframe anything into something positive.

Terrific by Jon Agee. 2017. New York: Dial Books for Young Readers.

Shipwrecked on a desert island, the world's biggest curmudgeon is stranded with an optimistic talking parrot who makes him want to surrender his pessimistic ways.

Theo's Mood: A Book of Feelings by Maryann Cocca-Leffler. 2013. Park Ridge, IL: Albert Whitman.

On Mood Monday, the children share their feelings about the past weekend. Theo has a hard time deciding how he feels. After listening to his classmates, he realizes he has multiple feelings.

Too Shy for Show-and-Tell by Beth Bracken. 2012. North Mankato, MN: Picture Window Books.

Sam is a quiet giraffe who has a lot to share at show-and-tell. Unfortunately, he is so quiet he is scared to talk in front of the class. He ultimately overcomes his fear and takes a risk so his classmates can learn more about him.

The Tortoise and the Hare by Jerry Pinkney. 2013. New York: Little, Brown Books for Young Readers.

From Caldecott-award-winning artist and storyteller Jerry Pinkney, this version of the classic tale can foster discussions about the value of perseverance. Slow and steady wins the race. Available in Chinese and English.

Trouble at the Watering Hole: The Adventures of Emo and Chickie by Gregg F. Relyea and Joshua N. Weiss. 2017. Resolution Press.

The forest animals are fighting with each other because their watering hole is too small. A bird and a bear cub work together to figure out how to solve the problem without fighting with each other.

Two Problems for Sophia by Jim Averbeck. 2018. New York: Margaret K. McElderry Books.

Noodles, Sophia's pet giraffe, has two problems: his kisses are sloppily wet and his snoring keeps everyone awake. Sophia's family tells her that she must solve these problems, which she cleverly does.

Unstoppable Me by Adam Dirks with Bethany Hamilton. 2018. Grand Rapids: Zonderkidz.

Makana the lion loved to surf until the day she wiped out. Now she is scared to surf. Her friend helps her find her courage to try again and persevere.

What Do You Do with a Problem? by Kobi Yamada. 2016. Seattle: Compendium.
A child struggles with a problem that won't go away. The longer the child avoids the problem, the bigger it gets and the more anxious the child becomes. Things turn brighter when the child stops trying to escape the problem and faces it head-on.

What If? by Frances Thomas. 1999. New York: Hyperion.
A Little Monster is worried about the "what ifs" of life. His mother reframes his negative questions into positive thinking so that he can go back to sleep.

When Pigs Fly by Valerie Coulman. (2001) 2017. Self-published (Originally published in Canada by Lobster Press).
Ralph the Cow wants a bicycle, despite the fact that everyone tells him cows can't ride bicycles. Ralph shows everyone, however, that perseverance and a growth mindset triumph over negativity.

Nonfiction

Be Positive! A Book about Optimism by Cheri J. Meiners. 2013. Minneapolis: Free Spirit Publishing.
This upbeat book introduces children to ways of thinking and behaving that will help them feel good about themselves when they choose to see the best in life.

Emmanuel's Dream: The True Story of Emmanuel Ofosu Yeboah by Laurie Ann Thompson. 2015. New York: Schwartz & Wade.
In this real-life story, a boy is born in Ghana with a deformed leg, and most people think he has no future. His mother disagrees and teaches him to be positive. He triumphantly grows up to play soccer, ride a bike, and go to work to support his family.

The Feelings Book by Tod Parr. 2009. New York: Little, Brown.
This book features a wide variety of emotions through colorful, whimsical drawings. It's ideal for helping young children identify and cope with emotions.

She Persisted around the World: 13 Women Who Changed History by Chelsea Clinton. 2018. New York: Philomel Books.
The author shares brief biographies of women around the world who have broken barriers by not letting anyone or anything get in their way.

Talk and Work It Out by Cheri J. Meiners. 2005. Minneapolis: Free Spirit Publishing.
In simple words and an engaging format, this book reviews how children can use conflict resolution to resolve their disagreements.

The Value of Optimism: The Story of Amelia Earhart by Ann Donegan Johnson. 1997. La Jolla, CA: Value Tales.

This biography of the famous aviator focuses on the value of optimistic thinking in making one's dreams come true. "Modern air travel would never have gotten off the ground without brave optimists like Amelia Earhart. Her courage inspired many dreamers to believe the seemingly impossible is possible if you believe in yourself and try your best."

You Are a Lion!: And Other Fun Yoga Poses by Taeeun Yoo. 2012. New York: Nancy Paulsen Books.

Yoga helps children learn to focus, regulate their emotions, and self-calm, while improving their flexibility. You can use this book to teach children poses, then put it in the library area so they can use it as a resource.

Tools to Help Families Support Optimism at Home

We must return optimism to our parenting. To focus on the joys, not the hassles; the love, not the disappointments; the common sense, not the complexities.

—FRED G. GOSMAN

Without even being aware of it, parents show their children how to live their lives optimistically or pessimistically. When a parent gives up on a repair job, loudly exclaiming, "I'll never be able to put this back together!" the child hears, "It's not worth it. Some things are too difficult." On the other hand, when the parent perseveres and says, "That was a tough job, but I fixed it!" the child hears, "It's good to keep trying. Sometimes you have to work hard to succeed."

Parents with an optimistic approach to life may already model and encourage their children's optimism, but likely not with intentionality. As educators, you and your colleagues can help families understand the benefits of optimism and the need to proactively support optimistic thinking at home.

When you begin to consider ways to incorporate learned optimism in your program, it's important to include families in the conversations. You can do this in a number of ways, including through in-person meetings, workshops, and newsletters and by sharing information via digital means.

Some family members might even want to borrow your copy of this book to learn for themselves about optimism, its many benefits, and how to turn a pessimistic learning style into an optimistic one. But most families are probably too busy or preoccupied to read the entire book. To make it easier to reach all families, we have provided handouts summarizing key points about optimism and some activities (similar to those for the classroom) for you to share in print or digital format. In some of the activities, you will need to give families reference materials, such as a list of optimism-related books, the planning steps chart, or a music-and-movement backpack.

Each handout and activity begins on a separate page, making it easy for you to copy and share them with families. You might post them on your website, include them in newsletters, or use them as the basis for family workshops. You can distribute them over time and invite families to share their reactions, experiences, questions, and suggestions with you.

What Is Optimism? Why Is It Important?

Optimism and pessimism are ways of thinking about ourselves, our experiences, and the events in our lives. Optimists expect good things to happen—to themselves, to others, and to the world. Pessimists expect the worst.

Whether a person is optimistic or pessimistic is partly in our genes. However, about 75 percent of the traits associated with optimism versus pessimism are determined by where we grow up, our families, and our experiences.

Optimism can help us cope with life's problems. Being optimistic seems to make one healthy, wealthy, and wise. For young children, growing up with an optimistic approach is the foundation for a rewarding life. Here are some examples of the benefits of being optimistic.

- Optimists have healthier lives and are better able to survive serious illnesses.
- Optimism is linked to living a long life.
- Optimists are better able to cope with stressful experiences.

Your Child and Optimism

No matter their age, optimistic children have greater success in school. They are more likely to feel good about themselves, make friends with peers, solve problems, take risks, and learn from their mistakes.

In our classrooms, children learn about literacy and numeracy, explore science and nature, enjoy music and art, and have plenty of time for playful learning. We also nurture children's optimistic thinking because it will support their health, wellness, and academic success throughout life.

Children's experiences at our program are most successful when families are our partners. Young children pay attention to what their parents and other important adults say and do, and they want to be like them. Every day you are teaching your children about who they are and how to behave in the world. You help them learn how to get along with others, be kind, enjoy learning, feel capable, and solve problems. These are all related to optimism.

When we do optimism-related activities in the classroom, we will let you know and provide a similar activity to do at home. We love hearing about the children's experiences at home, so please let us know how it goes when you try these activities. You can email us photos, quotes, and short notes or just share with us at drop-off and pickup times.

Explanatory Style: How Optimists and Pessimists See the World

Optimism and pessimism are ways of thinking called *explanatory styles*. Your explanatory style is the way you interpret what happens to you. These personal explanations of both the good and bad events in our lives leave us feeling either helpless and pessimistic (a negative explanatory style) or capable and optimistic (a positive explanatory style).

When optimists and pessimists explain experiences to themselves, they think about whether the situations they face are permanent (ongoing and not likely to change), pervasive (affecting everything in their lives), and personalized (they are the cause of what happened).

- Optimists see bad events as temporary; pessimists see them as ongoing. Optimists see good events as long lasting, while pessimists see them as short term.
- Optimists see problems as specific to occasions or circumstances. Pessimists see unhappy events as universal and affecting everything in their lives. Optimists see good events as all-encompassing. Pessimists see them as having limited benefits.
- Optimists think they have contributed to their good fortune; they look for the causes of bad situations outside themselves. If, however, they are responsible for the problem, optimists look for a way to turn the situation around. Pessimists blame themselves for problems; they believe their good fortune is due to outside circumstances or other people.

Do you wonder about your own explanatory style? If so, pay attention to your reaction when in a difficult situation. Do you see it as temporary, a one-time event, and generally something you can handle and then move on? If this sounds like you, you most likely have a positive explanatory style.

On the other hand, do you feel helpless, thinking, "This is terrible. I'll never recover." Are words such as *always* and *never* part of your reaction? Perhaps you blame yourself, even when you could not have avoided, prevented, or stopped a situation. If this sounds familiar, you most likely have a negative explanatory style.

Whether we mean to or not, adults model their explanatory styles for children. If we use optimistic thinking, we help children become optimists, thereby supporting their health, learning, and success in life. However, if you model pessimistic thinking, your child is likely to think this way too. The good news is that optimism can be learned—by both children and adults. We can refer you to resources to help you learn more about enhancing or changing your explanatory style and about supporting your child's development of optimistic thinking.

Helping Your Child Develop an Optimistic Explanatory Style

Optimism researchers agree: optimism can be learned and practiced until it is second nature. A wealth of research concludes that optimism makes us healthier, happier, and more successful in both school and life. Everyone can benefit from being more optimistic. We can do that for ourselves, and we can help our children become optimistic thinkers. Here are some things you can do to influence your child's explanatory style:

- *Model a positive, optimistic explanatory style.* You are your child's role model for optimistic thinking. To do this, try having a lighthearted approach to everyday problems and challenges the family is facing: "Whoops! Bowser grabbed tonight's dinner off the kitchen counter. We'll just have to have breakfast for dinner tonight. Who wants to help make the pancakes?"
- *Replace your own negative thoughts with positive ones.* Do this aloud so your child can hear your thinking: "I thought Hazel the puppy had taken my slippers, but then I remembered I had put them in the closet, out of her reach." When your child does this too, comment on what you saw or heard: "You were going to say, 'Oh no,' but you changed it to 'Oh well.' That's positive thinking!"
- *Accept your child's mistakes and challenges as typical parts of life.* Use humor, suggest how to fix a problem, and join in with help: "Whoops! I think your superstrong elbow accidentally bumped into the box and made the beads fall on the floor. I can help you pick them up. Let's see who can find the most beads. Look, there are some under the table."
- *Feed your spirit.* With your child, spend time doing things that give life some meaning. You might make music or sing together, take a walk in nature, practice your faith, express thanks, and so on.
- *Notice and comment on your child's efforts.* This helps your child see herself as a capable person: "I see you matched all the socks in the laundry basket. Now it will be easy to put them away."
- *Acknowledge stressful events that affect your family.* Provide age-appropriate facts about the situation and how long it will last: "Today our wonderful Nonny died in her sleep after being sick for a long time. We can talk with each other about how much we appreciated having her in our lives."

Nearly everyone can improve their future if they learn how to turn pessimism into optimism. Ideally, this process can begin during the preschool and kindergarten years, when children are still forming their explanatory styles. This will allow them to reap the overwhelming benefits of optimism. The earlier a child learns to be optimistic, the more long lasting the benefits of optimism will be.

Encouraging Your Child's Positive Outlook

When adults demonstrate a positive outlook on life, children notice and learn how too. Seeing strengths and positives helps everyone handle life's challenges. Here are some ways you can share a positive outlook with your child. (Adapted from Reaching IN . . . Reaching OUT, The Child and Family Partnership 2012.)

- Point out your child's positive behavior and strengths.
  - "You and Tyrone found a way to share the markers. Now you can both draw pictures and have fun together!"
  - "We had to wait a long time for the bus. It's hard to wait, and you were very patient."
- Comment on the positives in daily events.
  - "It's hard to get up early in the morning, but it gives us plenty of time to get ready."
  - "I'm looking forward to going to the park with you. Maybe we will see the chess players again."

- Talk about things you enjoy.
  - "I love baked beans. What is one of your favorite foods?"
  - "I like working on puzzles with you."
- Express your own positive feelings.
  - "I feel happy about cuddling on the couch with you alongside a pile of picture books to read."
  - "I felt good when I . . . [fixed the cabinet door, finished the laundry, etc.]"
- Ask your child to find the positives.
  - "What happened today that made you feel happy?"
  - "Tell me three helpful things you did today."

Tell an Optimistic Story (Activity)

Reading and discussing stories help children learn about lots of things, including facing and overcoming challenges through optimistic thinking. Tell or read aloud the story below. At the end of the story, ask your child what Jiang might do to face the challenge. Ask follow-up questions and guide the conversation toward an optimistic conclusion to the story.

Jiang Doesn't Feel Well

One day Jiang wakes up with a headache and a scratchy throat. His mom, Mrs. Chan, feels his forehead and says, "You seem hot."

"I'm not sick," Jiang says. "I'm going to ride trikes with Kevin today at school."

Jiang's mom takes his temperature. She says, "Just as I thought—you do have a temperature. We need to get to Dr. Maritza's office by eight."

Jiang grumbles most of the way to the doctor. "I always get sick. Why am I sick? I feel better now. I want to go to school."

But by the time they arrive, Jiang is quiet and looking very tired. The nurse hurries Jiang and his mom into an exam room.

Dr. Maritza comes in and asks Jiang, "What's wrong today?"

"I'm just a little warm," Jiang says. "I can go to school."

"I think he might have strep throat," Mrs. Chan says.

Dr. Maritza orders a quick strep test. The results are positive—Jiang does have strep throat.

"I'm never going to get to go to school again!" Jiang says. "Kevin will find a new friend. I won't have anyone to play with!"

Follow-up Questions

- What do you think Jiang is thinking in his head right now? Why does he feel that way?
- How can Jiang relax so he can get better?
- What do you think his mom should say to him?
- Do you think Kevin will still be his friend?

Guiding the Conversation toward Optimism

- What could you say to Jiang to help him feel less frustrated and angry? (Reassure him that he will feel better soon. Remind him of happy times he's had with Kevin and other friends.)
- What can Jiang do while he is getting better that might make him feel happier? (He can draw pictures while resting in bed, or he could send Kevin a note.)
- How can you reassure Jiang that the situation is not permanent? (In a few days, Jiang will feel better. He can then go back to school and play with Kevin.)

Next Steps

Make up a new story. This time you can make it about something that happened to your child. If there wasn't an optimistic ending in real life, figure out one now.

Put on a Play about Optimism (Activity)

Acting out stories about optimism helps children learn how to handle challenges using a positive explanatory style. Select three puppets, dolls, or stuffed animals to be the child, the parent, and the narrator in the script below. Have your child act out the role of the child as you act out the other two roles. Invite other family members to be the audience and, if possible, to record the show on a smartphone. After the play, ask follow-up questions to help your child understand the optimistic message.

Graham Wants to Finish His Puzzle

Narrator: Graham, please introduce yourself.

Graham: I'm four and a half years old. I live with my mom, my dad, my sister, and my cat, Bangles. I like to do puzzles.

Narrator: Graham sits at the table working on a new puzzle.

Mom: Hi, Graham. It's time to get ready for skating.

Graham: (*Makes a sad face.*)

Mom: Graham, you look sad. I thought you liked skating. What are you thinking to yourself?

Graham: I'm doing my puzzle, but now I have to get ready for skating. I'll never get to finish the puzzle!

Mom: It sounds like you're frustrated. You like skating, but right now you'd prefer to stay here and do your puzzle. It's hard to stop when you are having fun—even when it's to do something else you like.

Graham: I'm frustrated. I want to finish this puzzle now.

Mom: I know you would like to finish the puzzle now, but it is time for skating. Remember last week when you had to stop playing with your pirate ship? When we got back, you had time to play with it before dinner. You can finish the puzzle after skating. Now it's time to put on your boots and coat.

Graham: Okay. I'll finish later.

Narrator: Looks like Graham understands he can finish later. Things aren't always as bad as they seem.

Follow-up Questions

- What was Graham's problem? How did he feel?
- What did his mom say to help him talk about what was bothering him?
- What did his mom say to help him see that things are not always as bad as they seem?

Next Steps

Put on another play, this time from your child's own life. Ask your child to think of a time when he or she had a problem. Use the play to talk about what happened and how it was resolved.

Read and Talk about Books with Optimistic Themes (Activity)

At our program, teachers often read children's books as a way to teach optimistic thinking. When children see how a character succeeds by making optimistic choices, they have a model for their own behavior.

Choose an optimism-related book from the provided list to read over and over with your child. The first time you look at the book together, read it aloud, all the way through. Then read the book together again. This time, stop to ask questions about what happened, working with your child to figure out what might have caused the problem.

Discuss What Happened in the Book

1. Talk about what the main character did and said. What choices does he or she make? Does the character react to facts or fears? How can he or she resolve the problem optimistically? Here are examples of questions you might ask, inserting the character's name in the blank spaces.

   a. What happened to _____ in this story?
   b. How did this make _____ feel?
   c. What do you suppose _____ was thinking inside his/her head?
   d. What would you say to _____?
   e. What would you have suggested that _____ do?
   f. How did _____ think things through?
   g. What plan did _____ come up with?
   h. Why do you think _____ kept on trying?
   i. What do you think will happen next time _____ has a problem?
   j. Would you like to have a friend like _____? Why or why not?
   k. Would you have ended the story like this? If not, how would you end the book? Why did you pick this ending?

2. Remind your child of ways they are similar to and different from the main character. For example, compare their skills and interests. Focus on how optimistic thinking makes life better.

Next Steps

Repeat this activity using another optimism-related book from the provided list. Alternatively, ask your local children's librarian for a suggestion, or pick a favorite from your home library. You might want to try your hand at writing your own optimism-related book along with your child that you can then read together over and over again.

Plan, Do, Succeed (Activity)

The children in our class are learning to think and plan before they do a project. When children don't plan, they can get frustrated—and might turn to pessimistic thinking. To help your child learn how to plan before doing, read the following story about Marcella's planning process.

Marcella Plans to Build a Stable

Marcella, age five, is playing with her rubber horses. She gets an idea. "I want to build a stable for my ponies," she tells her dad.

"That's an interesting idea," he says. "What do you need to build it?"

"Maybe the shoe boxes in my closet," Marcella suggests.

"Hmm," her dad says. "But we use those boxes to store your shoes when you're not wearing them."

Marcella feels frustrated. She wants to build the stable.

"What else could you use to make a stable?" her dad asks.

Marcella thinks about what's in her baby brother's room. "I could use a giant diaper box. The one in Levi's closet is almost empty."

Her dad approves of her idea. Then he asks, "What else do you need?"

Marcella thinks again. She decides to use supplies in her art box.

Next her dad asks if she needs any help. Marcella answers, "Yes, please. Can you help me cut holes in the box so the ponies can look outside?"

"Sure," he says. "I'll show you a safe way to cut the holes."

Marcella and her dad work on the stable for a long time. When her mom comes home from work, Marcella shows it to her.

"Come see my stable, please. I've been working on it all day!"

Next Steps

Use the steps in the planning chart we provided to review Marcella's planning process. Afterward, have your child develop his or her own plan, using Marcella's story as an example. Consulting the steps in the planning chart, ask questions to help your child think about what is needed to carry out the idea. For example, "What materials do you need? Do we have them on hand? How long do you think it will take to do this? Can we do it all today or over a few days? What help might you need? Is this a job for one person or more than one person?"

Combine Art with Optimism (Activity)

Art is a way to express ideas and feelings, including optimism. With this activity, children may draw, paint, make a collage, or create a sculpture to tell a story. Others might explore colors, textures, and patterns instead of making something.

Create an Art Place

- Choose a place at home where it's okay for your child to do art. Stock up on supplies your child can use without supervision. You might have paper, markers, crayons, playdough and utensils, glue, safety scissors, felt and yarn, old catalogs or magazines, and so on. Supplies can be in a container or basket, or on a shelf within your child's reach. With this setup children can use the art supplies on their own, promoting independence.
- Read a book together about how colors and art convey feelings. Some suggestions are *My Many Colored Days* by Dr. Seuss (1996), *How Is Mona Lisa Feeling?* by Julie Merberg (2010), and *Niko Draws a Feeling* by Bob Raczka (2017). Discuss how you each feel when looking at the colors and illustrations in the book.
- Ask your child to create something that shows emotions, such as "I feel good about myself," "I solved a problem," "I had fun," "I am so happy," or "I did it all by myself."
- Join your child in creating something that shows how you feel.
- Talk with your child about what you each made and how each creation makes you feel.

Share the Art

- Hang your child's creations at home, placing them at a height where the child can see and appreciate them. If you like, frame them using strips of colored paper or inexpensive frames.
- Have your child dictate a description of her art and the feelings it expresses. Write these words on a sentence strip and post them underneath the artwork.
- Encourage your child to show and talk about his art with other family members. Visitors can note the positive, optimistic feelings the artist has conveyed.

Next Steps

- Express positive feelings with your child through dance, movement, and music. Ask questions and make suggestions to get things started: "What does happiness sound like when played on a drum? Can you do a happy dance? Shall we move like we are excited to be playing together?"
- Borrow the music-and-movement backpack from your child's teacher and use the contents in your home for dance, movement, and music activities.

Make Optimism Part of Every Day (Activity)

At the end of every day in our classroom, we spend a few minutes thinking about positive things. Children learn that even though life has problems and obstacles, there is always something good to celebrate. (This activity is based on an idea from Karen Reivich's 2010 *Fishful Thinking* podcast episode on cultivating optimism: www.blogtalkradio.com /fishfulthinking/2010/05/24/think-positive.)

Create and Use a Gratitude Journal

1. Use a notebook or make a journal by stapling a construction paper cover to some paper pages. Ask your child to decorate the cover with his or her name and a picture of something positive. Add your own name to the cover too.

2. Plan how and when to make an entry in the journal, such as in the morning before school, after dinner, or at bedtime. You might say, "This is a book we can draw and write in every day. We will each think about the day, then tell each other about a few good things that happened to us and to our friends. I will write them in the journal and read them back to you."

3. Model how to think, write, and share positive memories. Then ask your child to do the same. Offer prompts if needed. "Remember how when you got to school, Kaia was there already and you hugged each other?" Everyone's memories will be unique, of course. Here are some examples:

    a. I tried a piece of mango at snacktime, and I liked it.

    b. I helped Lucas put on his shoes.

    c. I remembered to use my napkin at dinnertime.

    d. It was Taco Tuesday!

    e. I fed Offeo all by myself.

4. Before writing about the new day, read a few positive memories from previous days.

5. Read the new journal entry at bedtime. Your child can think about the good things that happened during the day while falling asleep.

Next Steps

1. Invite other family members to use the gratitude journal too. Once a week when gathered at dinnertime, go through the positive memories together as a family. This reinforces the importance of looking for the good things in life. You could even include family members who live in another town or country by using a video conferencing app.

2. When you get to the end of the journal, start another one. Record the dates for each completed journal and keep them in a safe place.

3. Once a year or so, take out a journal and revisit your positive experiences with your child and family.

Learned Optimism Resources

Ben-Shahar, Tal. 2014. *Choose the Life You Want: The Mindful Way to Happiness.* Reprint, New York: The Experiment.

Borba, Michele. 2016. *UnSelfie: Why Empathetic Kids Succeed in Our All-About-Me World.* New York: Touchstone.

Brock, Annie, and Heather Hundley. 2017. *The Growth Mindset Playbook: A Teacher's Guide for Increasing Student Achievement.* Berkeley, CA: Ulysses Press.

Cairone, Karen B., and Mary Mackrain. 2012. *Promoting Resilience in Preschoolers: A Strategy Guide for Early Childhood Professionals,* 2nd ed. Villanova, PA: Devereux Center for Resilient Children.

Center for Healthy Minds. University of Wisconsin-Madison. 2017. *A Mindfulness-Based Kindness Curriculum for Preschoolers.* https://centerhealthyminds.org /join-the-movement/sign-up-to-receive-the-kindness-curriculum.

Colker, Laura J. 2010. "Teaching Preschoolers to Think Optimistically." *Teaching Young Children* 4 (1): 20–23.

Dweck, Carol S. 2008. *Mindset: The New Psychology of Success.* New York: Ballantine Books.

Duckworth, Angela. 2016. *Grit: The Power of Passion and Perseverance.* New York: Scribner.

Ferrucci, Piero. 2016. *The Power of Kindness: The Unexpected Benefits of Leading a Compassionate Life.* 10th anniversary ed. New York: Tarcher Perigee.

Fox, Elaine. 2012. *Rainy Brain, Sunny Brain: How to Retrain Your Brain to Overcome Pessimism and Achieve a More Positive Outlook.* New York: Basic Books.

Fredrickson, Barbara L. 2009. *Positivity: Top-Notch Research Reveals the Upward Spiral That Will Change Your Life.* New York: Crown.

Froh, Jeffrey J., and Giacomo Bono. 2014. *Making Grateful Kids: The Science of Building Character.* West Conshohocken, PA: Templeton Press.

Gates, Bill, and Melinda Gates. 2014. "Fusing Optimism with Empathy." *Stanford Report.* https://news.stanford.edu/news/2014/june/gates-commencement -remarks-061514.html.

Greenland, Susan Kaiser. 2010. *The Mindful Child: How to Help Your Kid Manage Stress and Become Happier, Kinder, and More Compassionate.* New York: Free Press.

Griffith, Owen M. 2016. *Gratitude: A Way of Teaching.* Lanham, MD: Rowman and Littlefield.

Harvard Medical School. 2008. "Optimism and Your Health." *Harvard Health Publishing* (blog). May 2008. www.health.harvard.edu/heart-health/optimism -and-your-health.

Howells, Kerry. 2012. *Gratitude in Education: A Radical View.* Boston: Sense Publishers.

Jennings, Patricia A. 2015. *Mindfulness for Teachers: Simple Skills for Peace and Productivity in the Classroom.* New York: W. W. Norton.

Lyubomirsky, Sonja. 2008. *The How of Happiness: A Scientific Approach to Getting the Life You Want.* Reprint, New York: Penguin.

MacDonald, Lucy. 2014. *You Can Be an Optimist: Change Your Thinking, Change Your Life.* London: Watkins Publishing.

Pearson, Jennifer, and Darlene Kordich Hall. 2017. *RIRO Resiliency Guidebook.* Reaching IN . . . Reaching OUT (RIRO). Toronto: First Folio Resource Group. www.reachinginreachingout.com/documents/GUIDEBOOK -MAY29-17-FINAL2_000.pdf.

Pritchett, Price. 2007. *Hard Optimism: How to Succeed in a World Where Positive Wins.* New York: McGraw-Hill.

Random Acts of Kindness Foundation. 2018. *Kindness in the Classroom Lesson Plans.* Accessed November 5. www.randomactsofkindness.org/for-educators #grade_k.

Reivich, Karen, and Andrew Shatté. 2002. *The Resilience Factor: 7 Keys to Finding Your Inner Strength and Overcoming Life's Hurdles.* New York: Broadway Books.

Ricci, Mary Cay. 2013. *Mindsets in the Classroom: Building a Growth Mindset Learning Community.* Austin, TX: Prufrock Press.

Rice, Judith Anne. 2013. *The Kindness Curriculum: Stop Bullying before It Starts,* 2nd ed. St. Paul, MN: Redleaf Press.

Sandberg, Sheryl. 2016. "Transcript: Sheryl Sandberg at the University of California at Berkeley 2016 Commencement." *Fortune.* May 14, 2016. http:// fortune.com/2016/05/14/sandberg-uc-berkley-transcript.

Sanguras, Laila Y. 2017. *Grit in the Classroom: Building Perseverance for Excellence in Today's Students.* Austin, TX: Prufrock Press.

Segerstrom, Suzanne C. 2006. *Breaking Murphy's Law: How Optimists Get What They Want from Life—and Pessimists Can Too*. New York: Guilford Press.

Seligman, Martin E. P. 2002. *Authentic Happiness: Using the New Positive Psychology to Realize Your Potential for Lasting Fulfillment*. New York: Free Press.

———. 2006. *Learned Optimism: How to Change Your Mind and Your Life*. New York: Vintage Books.

———. 2007. *The Optimistic Child: A Proven Program to Safeguard Children against Depression and Build Lifelong Resilience*. Boston: Houghton Mifflin.

———. 2012. *Flourish: A Visionary New Understanding of Happiness and Well-Being*. New York: Free Press.

Sesame Workshop. 2017. "Kindness Curriculum." *Sesame Workshop*. http://kindness.sesamestreet.org/view-the-results.

Sharot, Tali. 2011. *The Optimism Bias: A Tour of the Irrationally Positive Brain*. New York: Pantheon.

———. 2012. *The Science of Optimism: Why We're Hardwired for Hope*. Seattle: Amazon Digital Services.

Sheakoski, Megan. 2015. "100 Acts of Kindness for Kids." *Coffee Cups and Crayons* (blog). January 12, 2015. www.coffeecupsandcrayons.com/100-acts-kindness-kids.

Tough, Paul. 2012. *How Children Succeed: Grit, Curiosity, and the Hidden Power of Character*. Boston: Houghton Mifflin Harcourt.

University of Pennsylvania. *Authentic Happiness* (website). www.authentichappiness.sas.upenn.edu/content/about-us.

Willard, Christopher, and Amy Saltzman, eds. 2015. *Teaching Mindfulness Skills to Kids and Teens*. New York: Guilford Press.

References

Association for Psychological Science. 2010. "Optimism Boosts the Immune System." *ScienceDaily*. March 24, 2010. www.sciencedaily.com/releases/2010/03/100323121757.htm.

Ben-Shahar, Tal. 2014. *Choose the Life You Want: The Mindful Way to Happiness*. New York: The Experiment.

Boniwell, Ilona. 2006. *Positive Psychology in a Nutshell*. London: Personal Well-Being Centre.

Borba, Michele. 2016. *UnSelfie: Why Empathetic Kids Succeed in Our All-About-Me World*. New York: Touchstone Press.

Brown, Brené. 2018. *TED-Ed Talk*. Video produced by The RSA. Accessed November 5. https://ed.ted.com/featured/BXaLcbG4#watch.

Busch, Bradley. 2016. "How to Be Happy: A Guide for Teachers (and Everyone Else)." *The Guardian*. December 9, 2016. www.theguardian.com/teacher-network/2016/dec/09/how-to-be-happy-a-guide-for-teachers-and-everyone-else.

Cain, Janan. 2000. *The Way I Feel*. Seattle: Parenting Press.

Chang, Edward C. 2000. *Optimism & Pessimism: Implications for Theory, Research, and Practice*. Washington, DC: American Psychological Association.

Colker, Laura J. 2010. "Teaching Preschoolers to Think Optimistically." *Teaching Young Children* 4 (1): 20–23.

Contie, Vicki. 2011. "Gene Linked to Optimism and Self-Esteem." *NIH Research Matters*. www.nih.gov/news-events/nih-research-matters/gene-linked-optimism-self-esteem.

Danner, Deborah D., David A. Snowdon, and Wallace V. Friesen. 2001. "Positive Emotions in Early Life and Longevity: Findings from the Nun Study." *Journal of Personality and Social Psychology* 80 (5): 804–13. https://doi.org/10.1037/0022-3514.80.5.804.

Dewar, Gwen. 2017. "Teaching Empathy: Evidenced-Based Tips for Fostering Empathy in Children." *Parenting Science* (blog). September 2017. www .parentingscience.com/teaching-empathy-tips.html.

Doris Day Animal Foundation. 2004. *The Empathy Connection.* September 2004. Washington, DC: Doris Day Animal Foundation. www.humanesociety.org /assets/pdfs/abuse/empathy-connection.pdf.

Dweck, Carol. 2014. "The Power of Believing That You Can Improve." TED Talk. Filmed in November 2014. www.ted.com/talks/carol_dweck_the_power_of _believing_that_you_can_improve.

———. 2015. "Carol Dweck Revisits the 'Growth Mindset.'" *Education Week* 35 (5): 20, 24.

Fischer, Mariellen, and Harold Leitenberg. 1986. "Optimism and Pessimism in Elementary School-Aged Children." *Child Development* 57 (1): 241–48. https://doi.org/10.2307/1130655.

Fox, Elaine, Anna Ridgewell, and Chris Ashwin. 2009. "Looking on the Bright Side: Biased Attention and the Human Serotonin Transporter Gene." *Proceedings of the Royal Society of London Biological Sciences* 276 (1663): 1747–51. https://doi.org/10.1098/rspb.2008.1788.

Frank, Robert. 2018. "Jeff Bezos Is Now the Richest Man in Modern History." Inside Wealth. *CNBC.* July 16, 2018. www.cnbc.com/2018/07/16/jeff-bezos-is -now-the-richest-man-in-modern-history.html.

Frederickson, Barbara L. 2001. "The Role of Positive Emotions in Positive Psychology: The Broaden-and-Build Theory of Positive Emotions." *American Psychologist* 56 (3): 218–26. http://dx.doi.org/10.1037/0003-066X .56.3.218.

Gates, Bill, and Melinda Gates. 2014. "Fusing Optimism with Empathy." *Stanford Report.* June 15, 2014. https://news.stanford.edu/news/2014/june/gates -commencement-remarks-061514.html.

Hall, Darlene Kordich, and Jennifer Pearson. 2004. *Introducing Thinking Skills to Promote Resilience in Young Children.* Reaching IN ... Reaching OUT (RIRO). Toronto: Child & Family Partnership.

Harvard Medical School. 2011. "In Praise of Gratitude." *Harvard Mental Health Newsletter.* November 2011. Cambridge, MA: Harvard Health Publishing. www.health.harvard.edu/newsletter_article/in-praise-of-gratitude.

Hecht, David. 2013. "The Neural Basis of Optimism and Pessimism." *Experimental Neurobiology* 22 (3): 173–99. https://dx.doi.org/10.5607/en.2013.22.3.173.

Hewitt, Deborah, and Sandra Heidemann. 1998. *The Optimistic Classroom: Creative Ways to Give Children Hope.* St. Paul, MN: Redleaf Press.

Hoogwegt, Madelein T., Henneke Versteeg, Tina B. Hansen, Lau C. Thygesen, Susanne S. Pedersen, and Anne-Dorthe Zwisler. "Exercise Mediates the Association between Positive Affect and 5-Year Mortality in Patients with Ischemic Heart Disease." *Circulation: Cardiovascular Quality and Outcomes.* 6 (5): 559–66. www.ahajournals.org/doi/abs/10.1161/CIRCOUTCOMES .113.000158.

Jablon, Judy. 2018. "Children Deserve Leaders Who Learn." *Leading for Children.* Accessed November 5. https://leadingforchildren.org.

Jacobs, Bert. 2014. "Why Optimistic Leaders Build the Healthiest Companies." www.inc.com/bert-jacobs/why-optimist-leaders-build-the-healthiest -companies.html.

Kamp, Jurriaan. 2013. "Are You an Optimist? The Test." *Huffington Post.* Published November 7, 2013. Updated December 6, 2017. www.huffingtonpost .com/jurriaan-kamp/are-you-an-optimist-the-t_b_4234395.html.

Kaniel, Ron, Cade Massey, and David T. Robinson. 2010. "The Importance of Being an Optimist: Evidence from Labor Markets." *NBER Working Paper No. 16328.* National Bureau of Economic Research. www.nber.org/papers /w16328.

Karney, Benjamin R. 2010. "Keeping Marriages Healthy, and Why It's So Difficult." *Science Briefs* (blog). American Psychological Association. February 2010. www.apa.org/science/about/psa/2010/02/sci-brief.aspx.

Kim, Eric S., Kaitlin A. Hagan, Francine Grodstein, Dawn L. DeMeo, Immaculata De Vivo, and Laura D. Kubzansky. 2017. "Optimism and Cause-Specific Mortality: A Prospective Cohort Study." *American Journal of Epidemiology* 185 (1): 21–29. https://doi.org/10.1093/aje/kww182.

Kozub, Stephan. 2017. "Take a Deep Breath—No Really, It Will Calm Your Brain." *The Verge.* March 30, 2017. www.theverge.com/2017/3/30/15109762 /deep-breath-study-breathing-affects-brain-neurons-emotional-state.

Larsen, Elizabeth Foy. 2018. "The Executive Function Skills Every Kid Needs." *Parents.* Accessed November 2. www.parents.com/toddlers-preschoolers /development/the-executive-function-skills-every-kid-needs.

Lift Education. 2017. "Growth Mindset for Adult Learners." *Lift Education.* October 11. www.lifteducation.com/growth-mindset-for-adult-learners.

Livni, Ephrat. 2016. "The Japanese Practice of 'Forest Bathing' Is Scientifically Proven to Improve Your Health." *Quartz.* October 12, 2016. https:// qz.com/804022/health-benefits-japanese-forest-bathing.

Lyubomirsky, Sonja. 2008. *The How of Happiness: A New Approach to Getting the Life You Want.* Reprint, New York: Penguin.

McKay, Sarah. 2015. "8 Ways to Encourage a Growth Mindset in Kids." *Your Brain Health* (blog). November 17, 2015. http://yourbrainhealth.com.au/8-ways -to-encourage-a-growth-mindset-in-kids.

Parashar, Fiona. 2009. "The Psychology of Optimism and Pessimism: Theories and Research Findings." *PositivePsychology.org.UK*. October 24. http://positive psychology.org.uk/optimism-pessimism-theory.

Park, Bum Jin, Yuko Tsunetsugu, Tamami Kasetani, Takahide Kagawa, and Yshifumi Miyazaki. 2010. "The Physiological Effects of *Shinrin-yoku* (Taking in the Forest Atmosphere or Forest Bathing): Evidence from Field Experiments in 24 Forests across Japan." *Environmental Health* 15 (1): 18–26. https://link.springer.com/article/10.1007%2Fs12199-009-0086-9.

Pearson, Jennifer, and Darlene Kordich Hall. 2017. *RIRO Resiliency Guidebook*. Reaching IN … Reaching OUT (RIRO). Toronto: First Folio Resource Group. www.reachinginreachingout.com/documents/GUIDEBOOK-MAY 29-17-FINAL2_000.pdf.

Peterson, Christopher. 2000. "The Future of Optimism." *American Psychologist* 55 (1): 44–55. http://dx.doi.org/10.1037/0003-066X.55.1.44.

Peterson, Christopher, and Lisa M. Bossio. 1991. *Health and Optimism: New Research on the Relationship between Positive Thinking and Physical Well-Being*. New York: The Free Press.

Plomin, Robert, Michael F. Scheier, C. S. Bergerman, N. L. Pedersen, J. R. Nesselroade, and G. E. McCleam. 1992. "Optimism, Pessimism, and Mental Health: A Twin/Adoption Analysis." *Personality and Individual Differences* 3 (8): 921–30.

Positive Psychology Program. 2016. "5 Ways to Develop a Growth Mindset Using Grit and Resilience." *Positive Psychology Program* (blog). September 20, 2016. https://positivepsychologyprogram.com/5-ways-develop-grit-resilience.

Pritchett, Price. 2007. *Hard Optimism: How to Succeed in a World Where Positive Wins*. New York: McGraw-Hill.

Quast, Lisa. 2017. "Why Grit Is More Important Than IQ When You're Trying to Become Successful." *Forbes*. March 6, 2017. www.forbes.com/sites/lisa quast/2017/03/06/why-grit-is-more-important-than-iq-when-youre-trying -to-become-successful/#4a53b91c7e45.

Reaching IN … Reaching OUT (RIRO). 2012. "Positive Outlook." *The Child & Family Partnership*. www.reachinginreachingout.com/documents/PARENT TIPSHEET-PositiveOutlook-OCT16-12-FINAL_000.pdf.

Reivich, Karen. 2008. "The Seven Ingredients of Resilience." CNBC. June 30. www.cnbc.com/id/25464528.

———. 2010. "Think Positive." *Fishful Thinking*. Podcast. May 24. www
.blogtalkradio.com/fishfulthinking/2010/05/24/think-positive.

Reivich, Karen, and Andrew Shatté. 2002. *The Resilience Factor: 7 Keys to Finding Your Inner Strength and Overcoming Life's Hurdles*. New York: Broadway
Books.

Rius-Ottenheim Nathaly, Daan Kromhout, Roos C. van der Mast, Frans G.
Zitman, Johanna M. Geleijnse, and Erik J. Giltay. 2012. "Dispositional
Optimism and Loneliness in Older Men." *International Journal of Geriatric
Psychiatry* 27 (2): 151–59. https://doi.org/10.1002/gps.2701.

Sample, Ian. 2009. "Psychologists Find Gene That Helps You Look on the Bright
Side of Life." February 24. *The Guardian*. https://www.theguardian.com/science
/2009/feb/25/optimism-brightside-gene-mental-health.

Sandford, Kathryn. 2019. *8 Reasons Why Optimists Are Better Leaders*. Accessed
February 5. https://www.lifehack.org/articles/productivity/8-reasons-why
-optimists-are-better-leaders.html.

Saphire-Bernstein, Shimon, Baldwin M. Way, Heejung S. Kim, David K. Sher-
man, and Shelley E. Taylor. 2011. "Oxytocin Receptor Gene (OXTR) is
Related to Psychological Resources." *Proceedings of the National Academy of
Sciences* 108 (37): 15118–22. https://doi.org/10.1073/pnas.1113137108.

Schwartz, Tony. 2015. "The Importance of Naming Your Emotions." *New York
Times*. April 3, 2015. www.nytimes.com/2015/04/04/business/dealbook/the
-importance-of-naming-your-emotions.html.

Segerstrom, Suzanne C. 2006. *Breaking Murphy's Law: How Optimists Get What
They Want from Life—and Pessimists Can Too*. New York: Guilford Press.

———. 2007. "Optimism and Resources: Effects on Each Other and on Health
Over 10 Years." *Journal of Research in Personality* 41 (4): 772–86. https://doi
.org/10.1016/j.jrp.2006.09.004.

Seligman, Martin P. 2006. *Learned Optimism: How to Change Your Mind and Your
Life*. Reprint, New York: Vintage Books.

———. 2007. *The Optimistic Child: A Proven Program to Safeguard Children against
Depression and Build Lifelong Resilience*. Boston: Houghton Mifflin Harcourt.

Seligson, Hannah. 2008. "Optimism Breeds Success." *New York Daily News*. May
7, 2008. www.nydailynews.com/jobs/optimism-breeds-success-article-1
.328859.

Sesame Workshop. 2017. "Kindness Curriculum." *Sesame Workshop*. http://kindness
.sesamestreet.org/view-the-results.

Sharot, Tali. 2012. *The Science of Optimism: Why We're Hardwired for Hope.* Seattle: Amazon Digital Services. Kindle.

Sheakoski, Megan. 2015. "100 Acts of Kindness for Kids." *Coffee Cups and Crayons* (blog). January 12, 2015. www.coffeecupsandcrayons.com/100-acts-kindness -kids.

Singer, Jack. 2018. "The Terrific Power of Optimism in Sports Success." *Dr. Jack Singer* (blog). Accessed November 2. http://drjacksinger.com/the-terrific -power-of-optimism-in-sports-success.

Tyrrell, Kelly A. 2015. "'Kindness Curriculum' Boosts School Success in Pre-schoolers." *University of Wisconsin-Madison's School of Education* (blog). University of Wisconsin-Madison. www.education.wisc.edu/soe/news -events/news/2015/02/03/kindness-curriculum--boosts-school-success-in -preschoolers.

Vélez, Clorinda E., Elizabeth D. Krause, Steven M. Brunwasser, Derek R. Freres, Rachel M. Abenavoli, and Jane E. Gillham. 2014. "Parent Predictors of Adolescents' Explanatory Style." *Journal of Early Adolescence* 35 (7): 931–46. https://doi.org/10.1177/0272431614547050.

Viner, Brian. 2012. "The Man Who Rejected the Beatles." *Independent.* February 12, 2012. www.independent.co.uk/arts-entertainment/music/news/the-man -who-rejected-the-beatles-6782008.html.

Wray, Maggie. 2015. "Why Optimistic Students Earn Better Grades." *Creating Positive Futures* (blog). October 12, 2015. http://creatingpositivefutures.com /why-optimistic-students-earn-better-grades.

Index